MW01202066

COTTON'S SEAFOOD

A CAJUN AUTOBIOGRAPHICAL COOKBOOK

Written & Illustrated by Jim LaBove

Foreword & Design by James LaBove

For Cora and Cotton

Cora and Cotton LaBove, circa 1932

Table of Contents

Foreword

Growing up, my brother and I were lucky to enjoy many more seafood feasts than our family's lot in life would otherwise have afforded us, had we not been Cajun. Our childhood summers were improbably idealistic Cajun adventures in miniature: Hard work in some ways, but otherwise easy and carefree, with everything always seeming to work out as planned. I didn't realize it at the time, but none of this was a happy accident of fate. It took my parents a great deal of planning and effort to fashion (what appeared to my brother and I to be) weeks of pure serendipity.

Seafood in impossibly high supply always factored into these good times, whether we went out and caught it ourselves (as was often the case) or we met up with family and friends who had done the same. When we had occasion to enjoy one of these huge "Cajun vacation" seafood meals, at some point I would inevitably feel my father tap me on the shoulder and remind me to never take this for granted, mirroring what his own father "Cotton" had told him in the last years of his life: This is impermanent, it is fleeting, so enjoy it with those you love while you can.

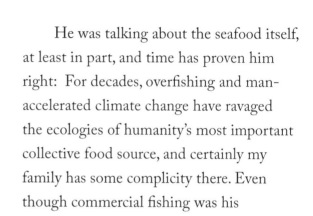

He was talking about the seafood itself, at least in part, and time has proven him right: For decades, overfishing and man-accelerated climate change have ravaged the ecologies of humanity's most important collective food source, and certainly my family has some complicity there. Even though commercial fishing was his livelihood (and without the benefit of modern science and hindsight), Cotton knew this: He could smell it in the air. And just as Cotton had done for him, our father wanted to instill in us a sense of gratitude and respect for the bounties that Mother Nature had provided us. But the seafood itself was not the only thing that he feared would be lost in our lifetime. The history of the people who settled in the unwelcoming land of coastal Texas and Louisiana, responsible for the very idea of "seafood feasts" (and certainly responsible for the physical transport and commerce of much of them) was also slowly drying up, as surely as the food sources that had sustained them for so long. It would be many years before I grasped the full import of what he was trying to tell me.

On some of these Cajun trips, we would gather with my mother's family at Grand Isle, Louisiana (a fishing and crabbing island community at the tail end of Louisiana Highway 1). Once we were there for a few days, with the cares of the "outside world" fading away for a while, I'd begin to imagine that reality started and ended between the two bridges that connected both sides of Grand Isle to civilization. It was easy to picture Kate Chopin's character Edna Pontellier walking along those same beaches, gradually feeling unmoored from the assignations that turn-of-the-century New Orleans society had thrust upon her. The area could have that type of effect on you. I remember feeling the weight of history and heritage upon me, even in the absense of responsibility that my youth (and my parents) had granted me on those magical trips. It felt natural, going out at the crack of dawn to bait traps for crabs, which would then be caught and eaten in all manner of wonderful ways for dinner later in the day. It felt like I was closing a loop of some kind, even if I didn't yet have the language to describe what was happening.

On other trips, we would spend time with Cotton and my grandmother Cora at their Sabine Pass home, or out on the water on the shrimp boat "Iron Eagle," in a manner not entirely removed from how Cotton would take my father out when he was a child. Sadly, I was barely old enough to remember the specifics of these boating trips – I would give anything to have more vivid memories of that time to hold onto. What I do remember clearly, however, was Cotton and Cora's love for us, and the mountains of delicious seafood that they would always pile in front of us when it was time to eat, constantly replenishing the fried shrimp, soft-shell crabs, fried fish, gumbo, etc. on our plates, even as we begged them to stop for fear that our tummies would burst. These family meals were luxurious in the truest sense of the word: We wanted for nothing. It felt like we were intruding, somehow. It shouldn't have been possible for folks like us to afford meals like this. Was this a miracle? Later on, I realized that it of course was.

Our family is not special or unique; at least, not more or less so than any other loving family. But the way of life that my father writes about in this book (and the heritage that binds so many of us together in Southeast Texas and Southwest Louisiana) has worth beyond the measure of the lives who lived it, and it should not be lost to the tides of time. The book itself is my father's message – to me, to my brother, to our future children, to you – written on driftwood and cast out into those tides, hoping for some eventual connection; hoping to keep our legacy alive. The events in this book happened, they were real, and on balance it was good. Our modern world may never afford people with the circumstances to have a lifestyle similar to my father's ever again, and that is likely good as well. But that doesn't mean we can't walk along the edge of the salt marsh from time to time, tasting the salt in the air and hearing the egrets cry, feeling somehow larger than ourselves despite the very tiny and personal corner of the universe we inhabit.

– James LaBove

"In the event that this fantastic voyage
Should turn to erosion and we never get old
Remember it's true: Dignity is valuable
But our lives are valuable too"
– David Bowie

Acknowledgments

"No man is an island" is a most appropriate quotation for the majority of man's endeavors; not the least of which is writing a book about one's past. An aging memory needs constant oiling, with reinforced knowledge of others who shared the barely perceptible blip that one's life makes on existence. I, therefore, have gone forward with the full knowledge that any good that I may do will most probably be "interred within my bones."

I could not have completed this work without the cooperation of my wife, Dodie LaBove, who put up with late nights spent at the keyboard or drawing table since starting this project in 2010. Dodie would proof-read my text many times, critique my drawings, and be supportive even when the drafts of my chapters were not particularly good, or my drawings lacked depth or perspective.

My son James wrote the foreword, designed the cover and undertook the exceptional typesetting, editing and design of the entire book, and encouraged me with my drawings, bringing them to life by the way he used them throughout the book. His artistic abilities made the book interesting and readable, and without him, there would probably be no book.

My other son Garret, brought the sober reality of marketing and research into the process of making a book; dealing with the publisher, copyrighting, Library of Congress registration and accuracy to the referencing of sources. Garret stepped up to the plate and took control of a portion of the making of a book for which authors are ill-equipped. It was Garret's constant insistence on quality control that kept making the book better.

My sister, Billie Faye (LaBove) Taylor, or "Billafay" as she is known, supplied details which I had forgotten about Mama and Daddy, and recipes that I did not have, as well as assistance with interpolations of the ingredients for those that neither of us had in written form. She also supplied pictures that I had thought were lost, and gave permission for us to use them in the book. My first cousin, Joyce LaBove, the only daughter (and only remaining living child) of my Uncle George and Aunt Rita LaBove (see Chapter 17, Keith Lake), supplied fine-tuning to incidents of my youth around Keith Lake (of which she was familiar), as well as details about my Aunt and Uncle's lives. Joyce, who we affectionately call "Joycey," also supplied pictures and gave permission for their use in the book.

Special thanks to a website operated by Louisiana State University called "A Cajun French-English Glossary." The site was created under the direction of Amanda LeFleur with the assistance of Benjamin Forkner. The website address is: http://www.lsu.edu/hss/french/ undergraduate_program/cajun_french/cajun_ french_english_glossary.php

Introduction

Now comes "Cotton's Seafood," an autobiographical cookbook that is not written about the young life of a world leader or a rock star, but rather that of a Cajun boy who was raised in the marshlands at the tip of the Louisiana/Texas borders; famous for absolutely nothing. Born to a family of fishermen, trappers and hunters who carved out a life in the marshy estuaries, this Cajun boy grew up in an environment that was alien to most people, even during that time. The average city dweller of today could not imagine what daily dangers and experiences were commonplace for the author. It is precisely that curiosity and sense of discovery which this book was written to address.

Although Cajun culture seems to be somewhat of a popular topic these days, there is a general misunderstanding as to the sub-currents that have always stirred the Cajun world. From the start, the *Acadiens* (French for Acadians, later to be known as Cajuns) encountered problems and prejudice. Like many expatriates of the Old World, the *Acadiens* came to the Americas for economic and religious freedom. And, like others of different ethnicities, they encountered anything but that. The "bullies on the block" at the time were the British, and the *Acadiens* did not waste any time becoming their "whipping boys." In a little less than 100 years, the *Acadiens* went from somewhat successful land-owning people in the lands around Nova Scotia to persecuted refugees deported from "pillar to post," ending up in south central and southwestern Louisiana – mostly because nobody else wanted this area and type of land.

They came to be known as Cajuns, and they carved out a rather unique life in what seems to have been a somewhat hostile environment. They even developed their own distinct dialect of

French. Though Cajuns were treated with suspicion and contempt even in their newly adopted land for much of the 19th and 20th centuries, in the 1940's and 1950's there began a resurgence and reverence of their history and past. Today, Cajun pride seems to be everywhere.

This new-found "Cajun craze" was further strengthened by the rise in popularity of cooking channels on cable television, along with the New Orleans Saints finally winning a super bowl. It seems that the world wants everything Cajun that it can get. Along with this demand, came a supply sometimes including "Cajun poseurs," who confidently profess to know everything there is to know about Cajun life and cooking. They often make roux that looks like cake batter, and their gumbo taste like it came out of a tin can. They overpower their dishes with too much garlic and pepper because they think that Cajun food is characterized by excessive seasonings, but in actuality nothing is further from the truth. For the most part, Cajuns (and especially the bayou Cajuns with which I am most familiar) used only the seasonings that they had available or could grow. Many of the seasonings that are used by these televangelical Cajun pretenders were not even available to Cajuns, and certainly would not have been bought by them if they would have had money (which was often characteristically in short supply for them). It would surprise most people to find out that there are many outstanding Cajun dishes that are surprisingly simple in their ingredient list. If you only listen to the cooking channels or recipe websites, you would be quite surprised to find that something can taste so good and not be absolutely drenched in every seasoning known to man. As is true with many other ethnic dishes, when preparing Cajun cuisine, precise preparation is much more important than throwing everything in but the kitchen sink.

In addition to correcting the anticipated misinformation that has accompanied this increase in interest, regional differences also need to be accounted for in order to get a true picture of who Cajuns are and what they eat. One of the main goals of this book is to clarify some of the misconceptions caused by conflating different "kinds" of Cajuns; to that end, I have adopted two terms for Cajun peoples with distinct cultures and influences, and I have defined them according to my own understanding of the groups. Throughout the book, I will make reference to people known as "Creole Cajuns," who I define as being located east of Lafayette, Louisiana and more principally around the New Orleans area; and the additional designation "bayou Cajuns," used here to signify those Cajuns located within the southwestern section of Louisiana and the easternmost tip of the Texas salt marshes. While there is much shared history and culture between them, there are important differences between the two as well, especially in the preparation of roux (a staple of Cajun cookery). Of the two, I would fall in the category of "bayou Cajun." This book, therefore, is devoted to bayou Cajun cooking, and is sprinkled with moments of growing up with my family to provide context for my Mama's (Cora's) Cajun recipes. Cajuns are quick to laugh, love and cry (all at great volume), so what follows is a small peek into some of the causes of all that laughing, loving and crying.

"*Chere* – you know dat big spoon I got wit da brown handle . . ."

Throughout this book are recipes that are as faithful as possible to Cora's original methods, drawing on the recollections of myself, my family and my friends, and also based on surviving records from the times when they are available. One of the problems with accurately writing down Mama's recipes was her unique dictations to me during such attempts. Typically, during her quantitative descriptions, she would say "da big spoon half full wit the brown handle," or "my gumbo spoon almost fill up," which were rather difficult to translate into precise measurements. Mama did not seem to actually measure anything exactly which I can recall. With the help of my middle sister, Billy Faye (usually jammed together to be pronounced as "Billafay" when spoken by our siblings and cousins – a fitting nickname for a Cajun girl), I have done my best to remember, rediscover, record and testify to the love and generosity imbued in Mama's recipes. Billafay and I have spent our entire lives attempting to conjure up the same Cajun kitchen magic that Cora wielded with ease, as it greatly enriched our lives and left an impression on us that we still feel decades later. I am certain that, were Cora with us right now, watching you leaf through these recipes, she would encourage you to modify the recipes to suit your family's personal tastes; to use them as a foundation for creating your own beloved memories and traditions just as she did for us, although I am quite sure those would not be her exact words.

CHAPTER ONE

THE ACADIENS

The Acadiens

The evolution of the ethnic group known as the "Cajuns" has
its origins in the late 17th century, in what is now Nova Scotia, plus
eastern Quebec and parts of northern Maine. It was in these regions
(then called Acadia) that early French colonists settled and began their
lives in the New World. Hostilities with the British began in 1710
when they took over French Acadia, and escalated until the French and
Indian War (1756 to 1763 also referred to as the Seven Years' War).
Throughout this time, the Acadians (spelled *Acadiens* in French) never
agreed to sign an unconditional allegiance to Great Britain, and they
were a constant threat to the British. One of the key difference between
the *Acadiens* and the British was that of religion, with the British
being protestant (Church of England) and the *Acadiens* being Roman
Catholic. The French settlers formed militias to fight the British and
furnished supplies to French troops at the fortresses of Louisbourg and
Fort Beausejour during the times of conflict. The British responded by
deporting many *Acadiens* to Britain, France and other British colonies.
They went so far as to killing Acadien families, destroying their farms
and seizing their lands, often without making any distinction between
the *Acadiens* who had been neutral and those who had resisted British
occupation. Many families were split and sent to different destinations.
The deportation by the British became known as *Le Grand De'rangement*
(The Great Upheaval). Contrary to popular belief and legend, the
British did not banish the *Acadiens* directly to Louisiana. Much of what
is popularly known about the Great Upheaval came from a fictional
account of the historic event by the American poet Henry Wadsworth
Longfellow, entitled "Evangeline," in 1847. In his long narrative
poem, Longfellow emphasizes the plight of the neutral *Acadiens* while
minimizing that of the ones who resisted the British.

Ultimately the British prevailed over the French, and in the Treaty of Paris in 1763 the *Acadiens* were provided a period of unrestrained emigration. It was during this time that some of the French settlers left the region and migrated to what is now south central Louisiana. Although the Louisiana territory was ceded to Spain in 1762 (and thus was under Spanish rule), the *Acadiens* were allowed to settle in the area and to retain their language, religion and culture.

The first group of settlers to come to Louisiana was led by a popular fighter and militiaman known as Joseph Broussard. After settling in an area known as the "Attakapas" (where they shared the swamps, bayous and prairies with the Attakapa and Chitimacha Native American tribes), the new settlers wrote letters to their families scattered throughout England and France, encouraging them to come and join them in Louisiana. In a letter written by Jean-Baptiste  Semer in 1766 where he encourages his father to come join him, he says "you can always come here boldly with my dear mother and all the other Acadien families. They will always be better off than in France. There are neither duties nor taxes to pay and the more one works, the more one earns without doing harm to anyone."

Many of the deported and displaced *Acadiens* eventually came to the Louisiana territory, where they settled in southern and southwestern Louisiana. There, the *Acadiens* mixed with many other ethnic groups to form the Cajuns of today. One of the obvious results of the cultural mixing by the *Acadiens* is the variety of surnames that are common among the Cajun population. The surnames of the original settlers of Louisiana have been augmented to include both French and non-French family names, causing the spelling of many to change over time. An additional factor in the name changes was the fact that many of Cajun people lacked education, leading to family names being altered over the years by various clerks and other recording agents in the course of business and regulatory activities. The spelling of my own family name, LaBove, is thought to have originated from LeBoeuf.

Although there are numerous theories to the contrary, it is generally accepted that the term "Cajun" evolved from the word "Cadien" which itself evolved from the term "Acadien." The Cajuns speak a unique dialect of the French language and have developed their own cultural traits. There were, however, numerous efforts to suppress the Cajun culture in the early 20th century, such as forbidding the use of Cajun French in schools. Cajun French speaking immigrants in Eastern Texas were looked upon with disdain, and were often either refused jobs or delegated to the lowest of occupations. In my own family, the speaking of French was greatly discouraged by my grandmother, Grandma "Jack" LaBove, who came to Eastern Texas around the 1900's, fearing that it would cause us to experience discrimination.

In the 1960's, however, things began to change. Groups like the Council for the Development of French in Louisiana were founded to preserve the French language and to encourage pride and appreciation for the ancestry of Cajuns. A state senator named Dudley LeBlanc who was called Coozan Dud (slang Cajun for "Cousin Dudley") led a party of Cajuns to Nova Scotia for the commemoration of the 200th anniversary of the Great Expulsion. Even the term "Cajun," which for many years was an insulting term, became a label of pride among

Louisianans. In 1980, the Cajuns were officially recognized by the United States government as a national ethnic group. This recognition came through a legal opinion in a federal discrimination lawsuit were it was stated:

"We conclude that plaintiff is protected by Title VII's ban on national origin discrimination. The Louisiana Acadien (Cajun) is alive and well. He is 'up front' and 'main stream'. He is not asking for any special treatment. By affording coverage under the 'national origin' clause of Title VII he is afforded no special privilege. He is given only the same protection as those with English, Spanish, French, Iranian, Portuguese, Mexican, Italian, Irish, et. al. ancestors."

Since music is such a part of the Cajun culture, the gaining of national attention in 2007 with the creation of the Grammy Award for the Best Zydeco or Cajun Music Album category was perhaps the final link of acceptance.

REFERENCES:

Brasseaux, Carl A., *The Founding of New Arcadia: The Beginnings of Acadian Life in Louisiana, 1765 – 1803.* Baton Rouge: Louisiana State university Press.

Brasseaux, Carl A., *Acadian to Cajun: Transformation of a People.* Jackson Mississippi: University Press of House.

John Mack Faragher (2005). *A Great and Noble Scheme: The Tragic Story of the Expulsion of the French Acadians from their American Homeland.* New York: W.W. Norton.

"A Letter by Jean-Baptiste Semer, an Acadian in New Orleans, to His Father in Le Havre, April 20, 1766. Translated by Bey Grieve. *Louisiana History* (spring 2007).

CHAPTER TWO

Cajun French & Cajun Slang

JIM LABOVE

Cajun French & Cajun Slang

I grew up listening to my grandmother, aunts, uncles and father speak Cajun French. My grandmother spoke French most of the time, especially when she was correcting us. Grandma Jack (as we referred to her) would not allow us to speak French, and was quite vocal in that regard on the few occasions when one of us made the mistake of answering her in French. When my grandparents crossed the Sabine River into coastal Texas in the early 1900's, French speaking immigrants were treated as if they were second class citizens. They were denied jobs in many cases and were often caricatured as being low class and uneducated. In truth, the majority of Cajuns were unsophisticated and unfamiliar with the ways of the outside world, owing largely to a self-imposed isolationism; this was itself a reaction to the years of turmoil they faced, beginning shortly after the arrival of the *Acadiens* in the New World and persisting all along the path that would eventually lead them to Louisiana. Ironically, Cajun French developed in large part due to Cajuns living at such a far remove from other cultural groups of North Americans at the time. Somewhat surpisingly, then, Cajun French is still spoken in some parts of south central Louisiana, including schools, even to this day.

Over time, Cajuns have mixed with English speaking people and developed an additional dialect that is part English and part Cajun French called Cajun Slang. Cajun Slang often uses English words in the wrong tense and syntax combined with Cajun French to make a sentence such as; "*Chere*, brought yourself up the bayou," which would mean roughly; "my friend, go north."

Throughout this book, I will sometimes use Cajun French, French and Cajun Slang terms that will be italicized to give you a taste of the Cajun culture. There are a few prevalent terms that would be helpful to know before we start. They are:

1. *Chere* – Cajun French – pronounced SHA meaning "my friend" or "pal" – a term of endearment derived from the French word Cher'.
2. *Cher'* – French -pronounced SHAR RE' meaning "my close friend" – a term of endearment usually used by a man speaking of his girlfriend.
3. *C'est si bon* – French – pronounced SAYE SI BONH' meaning "oh so good". Also can be si bon meaning "so good".
4. *Da* – Cajun Slang – pronounced DA meaning "the".
5. *Dis* – Cajun Slang – pronounced DIS meaning "this".
6. *Dat* – Cajun Slang – pronounced DAT meaning "that".
7. *Da utter* – Cajun Slang – pronounced DA UTTER meaning "the other". Sometimes, dis, dat and da utter are used in conjunction to poke fun at the way Cajuns speak.
8. *Coonass* – American slang – pronounced COON ASS – a term used to refer to Cajuns. The term "coonass" was originally a crass and somewhat bigoted term used by non-Cajuns to refer to Cajun people. Often proceeded by the adjective "dumb", non-Cajun people would use the term "dumb coonass[es]" to refer to co-workers, acquaintances and the like. Over time, many Cajun people have adopted the term, and will now refer to themselves as "coonasses" with some degree of exaltation. Only Cajuns would embrace a term of derision and use it with pride.
9. *Pooyie* – Cajun French – pronounced POOH YI' and sometimes POOH YI YIE' meaning "offensive" or "distasteful" and often associated with a smell or taste.

10. *Cooyon* – Cajun French – Pronounced COO' YONH meaning "dumb" or "stupid". Sometimes associated with (playful) correction of children.

11. *Up da bayou* – Cajun Slang – pronounced UP DA BA YOU meaning "north" or "go north".

12. *Down da bayou* – Cajun Slang – pronounced DOWN DA BA YOU meaning "south" or "go south".

13. *Cadien* – Cajun Slang – pronounced KA' DE IN meaning "Cajun"

14. *Canard* – Cajun French – pronounced KAH' NARd meaning "duck". Canard Francais – pronounced KAH' NARd FRON SAYE changes the meaning to "mallard".

15. *Chevrette* – Cajun French – pronounced SHA VRHETT' meaning "shrimp".

16. *Coco* – Cajun French – pronounced KO KO meaning "egg".

17. *Cochon* – Cajun French – pronounced KO SHON' meaning "pig".

18. *Pacane* – Cajun French – pronounced PA CON meaning "pecan".

19. *Poisson* – Cajun French – pronounced PWAH' SON meaning "fish".

20. *Farine francaise* – Cajun French – pronounced FAH RIN' FRON SAYE meaning "white flour".

21. *Farine de mais* – Cajun French – pronounced FAH RIN' MAYs meaning "corn meal".

22. *Poulet* – Cajun French – pronounced POOLe LET' meaning "chicken".

23. *Riz* – Cajun French – pronounced REE meaning "rice".

24. *Poul Deau* – Cajun French – pronounced POOLe DO meaning the name given to a small, duck-like water fowl common to the bayous and marshes of southeastern Texas and southern Louisiana. The English name for poul deau is "coot".

25. *Serpent Congo* – Cajun French – pronounced SERRa PHAH KON GO meaning "water moccasin". Water moccasins are venomous snakes that are a common threat to bayou Cajuns. Often, when I was a child, we shortened the term to simply "Congo" or "Kongo".

26. *Rat Mosque* – Cajun French – pronounced RAH MISKAY meaning "muskrat". The muskrat is a common animal trapped by bayou Cajuns for their hides.

27. *Qui* – Cajun French – pronounced KEE meaning "who".

28. *Boudreaux and Theroit* – this is my own Cajun Slang – pronounced BOOd ROW AND TER-REO, these are two typical Cajun surnames on the bayou. On occasion, when telling a joke or talking about the antics of Cajun life, the names Boudreaux and Theroit will be used to denote typical Cajuns.

When terms from the list above appear within the book, they will be italicized and the pronunciation and meaning will be repeated to give more context for their use. In describing the pronunciations, I have employed my own attempts at phonetics, which are almost certainly flawed but hopefully sufficient for the purposes of this book. This is not an attempt on my part to teach you, the reader, Cajun French; rather, it is an attempt to flavor the text with a small taste of our culture. Cajun French is a gentle language that flows well off of the tongue. If you wish to explore Cajun French in greater detail, I would encourage you to search for the relevant website sponsored by Louisiana State University (LSU); it provides a larger glossary of Cajun French terms acompanied by (what likely goes without saying are) much more scholarly pronunciations.

CHAPTER THREE

A Word About Being Cajun

A Word About Being Cajun

How Cajun do you want to be? Although being Cajun has become somewhat "campy" of late, care should be taken in pursuit of Cajunhood. As I've stated, my family are what I loosely refer to as "bayou Cajuns." Bayou Cajuns are from southwest and south central Louisiana, and were literally from the bayous and marshes. My family (like many bayou Cajuns) were in the seafood business, which entailed crabbing, oystering, shrimping and fishing; they also hunted and trapped alligators for meat and hides, along with *rat musque* (pronounced *ra' miskay*

Rat musque

and means muskrat) and the occasional *fouine* (pronounced *foo' ein* and means mink) for fur. There is actually very little glamor associated with being Cajun. The lifestyle is hard and challenging, and some of the foods eaten by real Cajuns can be challenging as well. To the average upwardly mobile suburbanite, some Cajun dishes would be considered absolutely disgusting.

It can safely be stated that Cajun foods were never designed with good health in mind. An example of this fact can be found in the boiled shrimp/crab recipe you will find later on in the book. As soon as the *chevrette* (pronounced *chev rhett'* and means shrimp) or crabs boil for the prescribed time, a Creole Cajun would turn the fire off and let the shrimp "soak" for 5 to 10 minutes. It is during this soaking period that the seafood and vegetables are said to absorb the spices. I am of the opinion that during the soaking period, what is mostly absorbed is actually the salt. Some Cajuns would argue this point (as most Cajuns would argue about any point); however, the majority of Cajun seafood dishes are rather salty. My father and I boiled shrimp in sea water when we were out on the shrimp boat. It was his contention that sea water had exactly the right amount of salt for boiling shrimp. In retrospect, I think he was right.

Another Cajun dish, alligator, has become somewhat fashionable in many eating establishments. It is often sought out and raved-over by the Cajun wannabes. I have eaten alligator many times, cooked many different ways, and despite the wisdom of the day I do not think it tastes "like chicken" in the slightest. I think that chicken tastes like chicken. I will concede that, when handled properly, alligator can be cooked acceptably (especially when fried), but poorly-prepared alligator can have poor texture and be extremely unappetizing. As a child, we had alligator dishes with some degree of regularity (since we hunted them), but there was never any extreme excitement in response to being told that we were having alligator for dinner. I suppose the point here is that being "a little Cajun" can be adventuresome and fun, but being "a whole lotta Cajun" is maybe more than the average American would bargain for. Philosophically, our family believed that if you killed an animal for any purpose, you had an obligation to use all or as much of that animal as you could, so as not to waste the resource that the earth provided you. Often times, that meant eating things that might be considered somewhat "earthy," to put it mildly. I am proud of my Cajun heritage and feel somewhat privileged to have experienced it. But, there are certain aspects that I am admittedly not in a hurry to re-live.

CHAPTER FOUR

I Remember Mama

I Remember Mama

My Mama, Cora LaBove, was born Cora Mary Ozio in the town of Franklin, Louisiana in 1916. Shortly after her birth, her family moved to Sulphur, Louisiana for a short period before finally settling along the Texas/Louisiana border around Port Arthur, Texas. She was a middle child of a family of four girls and two boys. Her father, Henry Ozio was a shipwright by trade, but the building and repairing of ships was not his true passion. Arriving in America as a young man from Italy, Henry was attracted to the Cajun lifestyle and became a hunter/trapper for most of the remainder of his life. Although he worked in the shipyards occasionally, the call of the bayou was strong for Henry.

Cora's mother was a member of a fairly well-to-do French family from New Orleans named Estelle "Stella" Toups. Estelle was born in America, although her family had immigrated from France. When Cora would talk of her parents, she would develop a glow that made her love for them quite evident. One of Cora's favorite stories was about the circumstances of her parent's first meeting. Forever the romantic, Cora's stare would trail off as she began the story, which she related in great detail, as if she were observing and relishing each moment. The story is set in New Orleans in the late 1800's, and it opens with young Estelle Toups preparing for her wedding (which was being planned and was not to Henry Ozio, whom she had not yet met). Although her family had lived in America for several years by this point, Estelle and her family only spoke French, which was customary for the times. As Estelle is busy designing her wedding dress and planning her wedding, enter stage left, a youthful Henry Ozio, a rugged, handsome Italian lad with a load of furs from his last trapping season to sell in the New Orleans fur market. Henry came to America as a youth and had been there for several years; although he

Cora at age 10, 1926

was dashing, he only spoke Italian. It was at this point in the story that Cora always started to become less detailed, preferring that the listener imagine for themselves how it exactly transpired. The denouement being that one week later, Henry and Estelle were married, and subsequently returned to the bayou Cajun life that Henry had come to love. Cora would relate to us that she could only imagine the fireworks display of love that must have occurred between Henry and Estelle that overcame the language barriers. Cora, the consummate story-teller, would always say that "love finds a way."

Cora grew up mostly in coastal Texas and met my Daddy, Cotton LaBove, when she was fourteen. They "courted" until she was seventeen, at which time they were married. She told us that Cotton was the only *prétendu* (pronounced *play thon diue*, meaning boyfriend) she had ever had. At the time of my birth, we lived in a house that was built by my father on a road between two small, coastal fishing villages on the Texas gulf coast. The area around our house was a marshland covered by salt grass and sea canes, and our closest neighbor was a good walking distance away. Being six years younger than my three older sisters left me rather alone, so I spent a lot of time with my Mama. We had a large garden because we raised almost everything that we ate, with the exception of the abundant seafood that was ever-present and provided by my Daddy. Mama and I worked in the garden every day for some amount of time, and she raised chicks that we called "biddies" to trade with at a general store in one of the villages. Mom would trade for bulk sugar, flour, coffee beans and a few other things that we could not produce ourselves.

Our garden was large, even judged by the standard of the times, and it required a lot of work to keep it maintained. Mama used to say that you had to plant enough to eat, enough to give to others and enough for the animals. Mom was an empathetic soul who saw value and worth in all creatures of the earth. I would imagine that city folk probably have a rather brazen view of the land and the raising and harvesting of animals, but Cora had developed a method of dealing with such things. She believed that all things on the earth had a place and a job. She would tell me that our job was to take very good care of all of our

Cora's parents, Estelle and Henry Ozio

25

animals and raise them with respect. When the time came for those animals to be harvested for food, it was our job to kill them as quickly and humanely as possible, and to see to it that nothing was wasted. To Cora, this was the grand play of life into which we were all cast.

Cora used to say, "everybody gets 10," then she would elaborate that some people get 6 of money and 4 of despair, or 7 of fame and 3 of sorrow, etc. but everybody gets 10. She would say that it was our job during our lifetime to develop a way to deal with the 10 that we were given. Cora felt that no matter how bad your life was or seemed to be, there was always someone whose circumstances were worse, and if they had somehow learned to cope with it, you could as well. If Cora had a philosophy, then I guess it was to accept the hand that life had dealt to you and to play those cards to the best of your ability. When life gives you deuces and trays, then you just have to bluff until the next deal.

Common to many Cajuns (but most probably because of the New Orleans heritage of her mother), Cora was superstitious, and believed in a Cajun offshoot of voodoo she referred to as "conjo." An incident that occurred between me and Mama when I was a young teenager illustrated to me the seriousness of her beliefs. When I was growing up, anytime that Mama (or anyone else for that matter) would drop any type of knife on the floor or ground, Mama would always step on it before it was picked up. It was her contention that if you did not step on the knife before you picked it up, you would be visited in the night by someone that you did not want to see. Although I do not remember

any further elaboration on the result, presumably this person would be there to do harm of some type to you. One day, while we were in the kitchen, Mama dropped a knife. As she was attempting to step on it, I grabbed her from behind and held her so that she could not step on the knife. I was laughing as I held her just out of reach so that she could not reach the knife, and this was all very funny to me. Mama began to cry, and it was at this point that I realized the seriousness of her belief in conjo. This incident made such a profound impression on me that from that day forward, I never teased Mama about any of her idiosyncrasies in this regard.

Conjo appears to be derived from the practice of voodoo, which is considered by some to be a living religion in the southern United States, and more principally in the New Orleans, Louisiana area. Voodoo bears some similarities to (and follows somewhat closely) the Catholic religion; specifically in the belief in saints and priests. One point of diversion was the fact that in voodoo, women played a leading role as priestesses, or "mambos" as they were called. In voodoo, the term "conjo" refers to "a magic charm made up of an assortment of things and often placed under the doorstep to gain some control over an intended victim"[1]. Early literature of the period sometimes refers to a "conjo woman," in some circumstance pointing to the fact that conjo did appear to branch off in some sort of way from voodoo. One of Mama's home remedies that we were given when we were sick bears a resemblance to (if not directly based on) a voodoo drink that was used to celebrate June 23rd, the eve of St. John the Baptist. The voodoo drink consisted of rum, sugarcane molasses and anisette, and that compared somewhat to Mama's remedy which was made with whiskey, honey and alum. We were given this "medicine" for many types of ailments.

Cora had numerous other small practices and beliefs that I encountered while growing up, and they could seem rather strange when considered out of the context of their place and time. Mama kept a small cloth bag containing a coin that was pinned to the inside of her bra so that she "would never be broke" in her life. The value of the coin was not significant since the coin was actually symbolic to the belief. Although she seldom encouraged us to do so, she actually believed that garlic worn in a small sack around your neck would make you well when you were sick. Cora believed that if you placed absinthe in your closet, it would keep away germs. When we had *fievre* (pronounced *fi en*, meaning fever) and colds, Mama would boil sassafras root to make a tea which she would mix with honey and whiskey and then give that to us. When we cut our fingernails or she cut our hair, she would gather all of the cuttings and burn them since she believed that people could take such things and use them to do harm to you.

Cora had some specific superstitions that were connected with Sunday. We were never allowed to iron clothes on Sunday, because if you did, you would be placing the hot iron directly on Christ or applying heat to Christ. We were never allowed to sew or use any type of needle on Sunday, because you would be pushing the needle directly into Christ or you would be sewing up Christ if you did so. She did not ever kill or clean chickens on Sunday either, but she did not explain the reason behind this belief. It's possible that this was derived from the significance of chickens used in many rituals in voodoo. There was also some significance to the cooking of black-eyed peas and rice at certain times, although I cannot remember the exact significance. Again, this could have come from the significance of

Bobby Lee and Billie Faye LaBove, circa 1940

black-eyed peas and rice ("congri" or "congris") being used in a ritual where it was either a lucky or evil charm depending upon the intention of the particular voodoo priest. All in all, suffice it to say that growing up with Cora was an interesting experience in this regard.

Because of the remoteness of our house and the fact that I was much younger than the youngest of my three older sisters, I had no one with which to play. Because of my early aversion to anything but *cabri* (pronounced *ka brie'* and means goat) milk, we had some milk goats, one of which was a pet billy goat named "Billy" (a name I thought of that was hardly Mensa worthy) that I led around with his head constantly under my arm. Billy and I were a topic of scorn by my sisters since Billy chose to enhance his appeal to the fairer goat sex by urinating on his head. Let us just say that Billy and I had a certain air about us, a *je ne sais quoi*, which set us apart from the mundane. Besides Billy and the constant smell of goat urine, I spent most of my very early life with my Mama, Cora.

Cora LaBove was a remarkable woman of many talents. I was constantly amazed by the process Cora would undertake any time she encountered a new item of interest. Any time that anyone would bring a new way of creating something to Cora's attention, she would immediately learn how to do it. As a consequence, Cora became adept at many things, including sewing, knitting, crochet, and other craft abilities that are too numerous to mention. She was so good at sewing that my older sisters preferred the clothes she made to "store-bought" items. Cora possessed a tremendous amount of stored energy (which today would likely be referred to as hyperactivity), and she could focus all of that energy on whatever project she was interested in at the time. She would also constantly be cooking at the same time that she was doing all of these other activities, for it was cooking in which Cora excelled.

Cora was a "man's cook," and her field of excellence was in creating hearty dishes that a man would want to sit down to and eat until ruination. With the exception of a few noteworthy dessert dishes that she did do well, Mama was not a brilliant confectioner. Her chocolate cake was always lopsided and the icing was too stiff, but I told her it was my favorite and I remember it to this day. I must admit that it was only my favorite because I loved Mama so much. It was actually rather dreadful to look at, but it did taste pretty good. She did have some brief moments of sugar-coated brilliance, because her pecan pralines were the best I have ever tasted anywhere (including New Orleans French Quarter). Cora's genius however, was in the cooking of main dishes.

Because of our large garden and our farm animals, we always had a considerable amount of very good food to eat. We also canned extensively. Although we had goat meat only on rare occassions, we always had goat milk and an abundance of chicken and pork since we raised hogs. We never had any cows, but Cotton would trade seafood for beef to friends that did raise beef cows. Our big "hole card" was seafood, which we always had in steady supply. Cora and I dried shrimp, and we also froze them in water for preservation. When fresh seafood is frozen completely immersed in water, it will maintain its peak flavor for more extended periods. We used this method to freeze shrimp, fish, crabs and oysters (all with successful results). I was Mama's helper for the canning of many vegetables from our garden. We would concentrate on one specific canned product at a time, spending the whole day or more preserving a year's worth of food for us with enough to spare to give to our friends and neighbors. I can still remember how sore my fingers were when we were canning peas where I would spend the whole day shelling them.

Cora got a sort of internal glow out of giving to others. I cannot define it, but I can still see her face as she was giving something (that she had worked on hours) to someone else. Cotton also had this certain "something," that he perhaps caught from Cora. For my whole life with them, I remember Cora and *Cottee* (pronounced *cot tee'* and was a name Mama used to refer to Cotton) giving away things they had worked for to other people who they felt needed it. I still cannot define it, but all I have been able to figure out is that it must have provided something, because they did it their entire lives.

REFERENCES:

[1] *"The Lexicon of Marie Laveau's Voodoo" by Beatiz Varela, University of New Orleans, page 4. In addition to the cited quotation, other related information was derived from this article.*

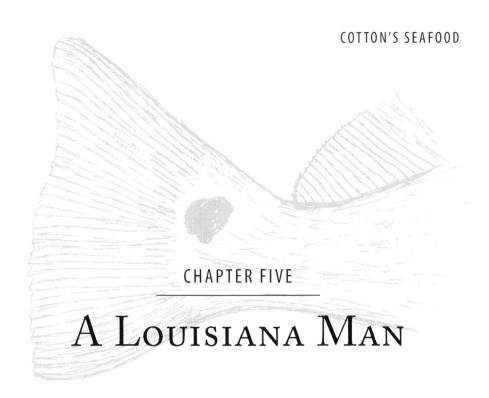

CHAPTER FIVE

A Louisiana Man

A Louisiana Man

My dad, Cotton LaBove, was a Louisiana man. He personified all that this entailed – a hunter, trapper, commercial fisherman and bayou personality. Although he could exhibit a stoic nature, he had a zest for life that was at times subordinated but always present. Like most twentieth century bayou Cajuns, he was at home in the marsh and on the bayou; he had learned to navigate the streets of civilization, but only to a point. The warmth of the bayou culture pulls strong on Cajuns, and they can only take so much of the outside world. When shrimping with Cotton on his boat as a child, I could see a look in his eyes that I did not see when he was anywhere else. He was at home on his boat – he was comfortable there. For better or for worse, Cotton is responsible for the man that I am, and I too cannot escape the tug of the bayou that I have grown to appreciate because of him. My biggest regret is that it took so many years for me to realize this.

Cotton LaBove was born Lazime LaBove on March 20, 1910 in a little bayou town of Johnson Bayou, Louisiana, which is located very close to the border with Texas and the Gulf of Mexico. To this day, Johnson Bayou is still largely unknown to most people from Louisiana except those living in relatively close proximity. Cotton was the middle male in a family of ten boys and one girl. Cotton got the name "Lazime" from his Uncle Lazime. The story goes that Cotton didn't really have a name for several days after he was born. His Uncle Lazime came to visit about that time and told Cotton's mother, "Eve," that she ought to call the young lad Lazime. Thus, Lazime was the name he received. One day while picking cotton, a very young Lazime went to sleep in the cotton field, and the people had a hard

Cotton in his early 20's

time finding him because of his white hair. From that day forward, he became known as "Cotton." Few people (including very close friends) ever heard or knew that Lazime was Cotton's real name.

Like most bayou Cajuns, for Cotton formal education was a luxury that was out of reach and did not apply to the way of life ahead of him. Cotton made it through the sixth grade, but he was forced to quit school to help his mother provide for the family since his father, Jack, was an alcoholic and poor provider. As a very young teen, Cotton's family crossed the Sabine River into Texas and settled in a small coastal fishing village known as Sabine Pass. Since the coastal marshes and bayous of this area were so similar to Johnson Bayou, Cotton was able to continue all of his bayou Cajun activities of hunting and fishing as well as to venture out into new areas and expand his vistas. Cotton would become a renaissance man, mastering numerous trades and skills including wielding, auto & diesel mechanics, carpentry and machinist, even attaining the rank of Master Electrician. Although he ventured into these areas during his early life, he never strayed far from his bayou roots, continuing to trap and fish throughout these times. Cotton considered himself a commercial fisherman and appeared to dismiss his other accomplishments. While growing up, I discovered that my dad was accomplished in something else: He could completely disassemble and reconstruct any piece of mechanical equipment that he encountered. When I would inquire as to how he knew what to do to repair a given item, he would reply that anyone who could take something apart could put it back together. He told me many times that once you take something apart, how it

works and what is wrong with it would be easily evident. He used to tell me that anybody could do all of the other things he had come to learn in his life. He was apparently unaware that he was talented in so many other pursuits and seemed to only value his abilities in the realm of commercial fishing and hunting. Cotton encouraged my sisters and me to pursue education, but he did not seem to value it for himself past the point of reading, writing and performing basic mathematics, all at which he was adequately accomplished.

Eve and Jack LaBove,
Cotton's parents

In 1933, Cotton married my mom, Cora Mary Ozio, and together they had six children. The first were twin girls who died at birth, then my three older sisters and me as the youngest and only male. All of their children (except myself) were born at home. Having children at home is not for the uninitiated. On Mama's first delivery, one of my twins sisters lived for four hours, and the other lived for about twenty hours. When recalling the time of the birth of the twins, Mama told me that the anguish and pain of carrying babies to term only to have them die right after birth was indescribable for her and my dad. Then, the additional burden of burying the twins fell on my father, since they lived in a time right after the great depression and this was how things were done during that era. When I asked my father about the burial of the twins I found myself struggling to even talk about it,

The LaBove family, circa 1949

much less being able to mentally place myself in the position of trying to empathize with what he must have felt at the time. As was usual for Cotton, his reply was calm and brief: He said that a man does not have the right to allow the problems of life to cause uncontrollable or disabling reactions. A man does what he has to do to take care of the people he is duty-bound to protect. He then changed the subject, because he was averse to dwelling on unsavory topics to which man has no control.

While working in various occupations, Cotton continued to hunt ducks commercially on horseback with his brother George in the Sabine marshes; he "floundered" (which means spearing or "gigging" flounder) the Sabine channel; trapped muskrats; hunted alligators; and he walked the front marsh and cast netted bull redfish in marsh potholes at low tides; all to make extra money. The thoughts and fears of the great depression were always on the minds of both Cotton and Cora, and they both did anything and everything they could to scratch out a living. When I was very young, I remember Cotton talking to me about the depression; about people starving to death, and the fact that there were very few jobs to be found. He seemed to be telling me that this was the reason that he knew how to do so much, since multi-talented people seemed to be the only ones who made it out of the depression with any type of life. Although my dad was somewhat of a stoic man of incredible strength, I sensed an unusual type of fear in his tone when he talked about the depression and what it was like to have lived in that time. In his eyes, I could see a blankness that reinforced that fear – a blankness that exuded a type of ingrained despair that accompanied long periods of unease and insecurity. It was the worst of times.

Jim and Billie Faye "Billafay" LaBove as children

When Pearl Harbor was bombed and World War II broke out, Cotton (like so many other American men) was moved to join the military, but he had too many children, so they would not take him. In an effort to do his part for the war effort, Cotton went to work in the shipyards, where his numerous skills were sorely needed. Cotton quickly ascended the ranks in the shipyard and even invented a modification to a type of clutch that was experiencing dependability problems. Cotton's boss in the shipyard contacted one of the larger engine manufacturers in Detroit and Cotton was taken to the plant to show his invention to the engineers. His invention was incorporated into the design and Cotton returned to his job without much more than a handshake. When he and I discussed the fact that he did not profit from the invention and basically had given it over to others, he replied rather typically (for Cotton), saying that it was not important in his life and that he was really anxious to get back to what he wanted to be doing. With the end of the war, Cotton was able to do just that: Get back to the commercial fishing and hunting that he loved so much. The pull of the sea is strong in men; that they "go down to the sea in ships." It was the best of times.

Since I was born about this time, my actual recollections were just starting to begin. I will spend my young life learning the many skills that Cotton knows and desires to pass on to me. I accept those lessons, sometimes reluctantly, as things that I probably will need to know, since I am not sophisticated enough to be fully aware of the scope and breadth of life's rigors. It seems that Cotton and I were constantly building onto our house, repairing the motor of the boat, fixing the truck, wielding, inventing a contraption to solve a problem, wiring a house, repairing broken appliances, or performing any one of these same tasks for our relatives and friends. Cotton, although he was oblivious to the fact, was a born inventor of a sort. Long before I had ever heard of a solar water heater (or before anything involving solar power) was a topic, Cotton devised a solar-powered shower for us. It consisted of a small room built out of drift wood lumber, which used to be in abundance on the beaches before the government clamped down on ships throwing dunnage or lumber used for shipping into the sea. On top of the small building, Cotton mounted a 55 gallon drum which he painted flat black and fitted with a pipe and water valve into the center of the room. In the morning, he would fill the drum about two thirds full of water and allow the sun to heat the water all day. Then, at the end of the day, he would finish filling the drum to cool the water down to the right level for showering. It worked so well that he later added a cold water line in just before the valve so that you could adjust the water temperature to exactly what you wanted. Since we did not have a hot water heater in the house I grew up in, Cotton's solar-powered hot water heater was even more significant, especially to us. Except on overcasts or the coldest of days, we used this outside shower for most of my youth.

I sometimes approached my tasks with Cotton with the expected reticence of any young person asked to work for which they see no purpose, but I suppose that was to be expected. I now realize that Cotton was passing on to me the things that have enabled me to accomplish what I have accomplished and made me the man I am today. I guess the great inequity of life is that the people to whom we all owe so much always seem to be gone by the time we finally realize their importance to us.

Cotton LaBove was both a simple and complex man. He did not have any bad habits that I was aware of, except possibly his agility with expletives. He did not drink alcohol or hang around with those who did, but he had no special convictions against such things. He actually enjoyed sharing an occasional drink and attending a *faye-do-do* (pronounced *fay' doe doe*, describing a *Cadien* [Cajun] musical get-together) but that was by no means the central focus of his life. He had no hobbies or outside interests other than my mother and his life on the water. He was not particularly religious, but he believed in integrity, charity and honest relationships in his business dealings and with his fellow man. When it came to work, there were no holidays or special days to Cotton. One of my earliest recollections of Cotton was him smiling as he watched us open up Christmas presents in our living room while he worked on his shrimping net. That was his idea of taking a day off. Cotton lived to work and worked to live.

CHAPTER SIX

CORA ON COOKING

Cora on Cooking

Cora's philosophy for cooking was rather novel as good cooks go. She believed that cooking did not involve a profusion of herbs and spices, but was rather an amalgamation of good ingredients in abundance and careful preparation. She always told me that cooking need not be complicated in its structure. She once said that the main ingredient of a dish should be the focal point, and there should only be a few flavor enhancers added. To Cora, the preparation was what actually made the dish come alive, and no amount of cleaning, chopping, stuffing, kneading or stirring was too much to achieve her goal. Cora had the energy of a Spartan warrior who had taken a job as a longshoremen. Standing a little over five feet tall and possessing hyper-energy, Cora could cook a complicated dish while cleaning the house, while assisting us process the catch, while bringing us something to drink while we worked, while waiting on customers for seafood, while... well, the list goes on. No matter what the activities were that made up her day, cooking was always involved in some way. She also seemed to be constantly canning produce that she raised in what seemed to be a perpetual garden, no matter where we lived. The star of Cora's cooking show was green onions, and there was always some to be found growing immediately out of the back door of our house (usually in an old wash tub that had outlived its usefulness as such and got drafted by Cora for garden duty). As a matter of fact, if something could hold dirt, it would usually get drafted for some plant that Cora used in cooking. We always seemed to have green onions, parsley, bird's-eye peppers, bell peppers, garlic and tomatoes growing around the house in Cora's makeshift pots. We always had a bed of asparagus, since Cora felt it was a good investment of time due to its longevity of production (up to twenty years). Cucumbers and broccoli were ever-present, but Cora had a nemesis: The dreaded lettuce. For some reason, she could not seem to get lettuce to come out right, but I'm sure that she is still planting lettuce somewhere up there, because if one thing that could be said for certain about Cora, it was that she was relentless when she endeavored to accomplish something.

Canning was of particular value to Cora, partially because she was raised during the depression of 1929, and partially because she relished having all of those gleaming jars of colorful foods lining the shelves of our back porch. She frequently said to me that even though we may not have any money, we had better food than the rich folks. Although I did not understand and exactly agree with her at the time, I now know that she was totally correct in her assessment; that her canned foods were properly prepared with no additives, and our seafood was eaten at the peak of freshness. The "rich folks" that Cora referred to, despite all of their money, could not get the seafood caught and prepared as fresh as we got it, and they would likely scoff at our canned foods in favor of their agri-business prepared foods. It seems that the world is just now catching on to something that Cora knew all along. The only way to get safe, good quality food is to grow it and can it yourself. Cora and Cotton both believed that seafood begins to deteriorate immediately from the point that it was caught. All of our seafood was heavily iced down while it was still alive, and kept that way up until the time it was sold to a customer or prepared for us to eat. On the occasions when we froze seafood for extended keeping, it

Cora and Cotton LaBove's children, circa 1948

had to be frozen totally immersed in water, with no part of the seafood exposed to air. Freshness is everything with seafood. Cotton used to say that the reason the seafood we ate tasted so good was because it "slept in the bay last night".

I suppose the main reason that food was so important to both Cotton and Cora was the fact that they were married in 1933, when the Great Depression was still omnipresent. Cotton use to tell us as children that he and Mama were lucky during that time because he had a decent job, and because they had a place to live and grow their own food. Cotton's "decent job" consisted of being a chauffeur and auto mechanic for a wealthy hotel owner, and Cora worked as their cook. For these services, they were given a place to live, a garden that Mama tended "on halves with the owner" and $5 per week, which

Cotton said was good money for the times. It was in this backdrop that Cora honed her canning skills. Cora could can anything, including cut-up chickens, stews, soups and chow-chows (Cajun salsa), in addition to the usual corn, beans, asparagus, etc. If you could name it, Cora could can it.

By the time I arrived on the scene in 1946, Cora was a canning pro with a complete assortment of canning wares. I was Cora's assistant at a very early age because canning was a wonderment to me. Cotton built a large, screened-in back porch that was rather narrow but ran the full length of the back and side of the house. All along the wall ran narrow, floor-to-ceiling shelves for canned foods. I can still remember walking along the porch, looking at all of the gleaming jars of food in every color imaginable. This was what Cora called our "general store," and it was constantly changing. As we depleted the jars by eating them or giving them to loved ones or neighbors in need, Cora and I would create new "products" to take their place. Mama always said, "you have to can enough ta eat and enough ta give," and give she did. I was constantly being sent to bring someone a few jars because they were on hard times, or because Mama felt that they or their children did not have enough to eat. That was just Cora's way.

Cotton built a complete outdoor work area for Cora to can. "Complete" in this case meant that it was functional, but not exactly luxurious. There were work tables and a rack to build a fire for heating the scalding water and pressure cookers. Cotton also had built various cooling racks and special-purpose devices to help in the canning process. I distinctly remember when he welded our first butane-fired burner for outdoor canning. Mama was very excited because it did not blacken the bottom of her pots, and it did not require constantly tending the fire and adding wood. I remember her saying that this was "the cat's meow," whatever that meant.

Cora on Stocks

Mama used stocks with some frequency in her cooking. Since we raised a lot of chickens when I was young, chicken stock was more prevalent in our household than it would have been in the usual bayou Cajun household. Mama often added chicken stock to her seafood dishes, with what I considered to be great success. Actually, bayou Cajuns did not use stocks to any great extent; more often, they would use water in their dishes that called for liquid. This, of course, goes back to the simple lifestyle often employed by bayou Cajuns where everyone in the household worked in the family business, whether it be shrimping, crabbing, fishing, trapping or hunting. The hours needed for cooking and watching a stockpot were simply not available, unless there was an activity with which it could be combined.

If you listen to the TV chefs on the cooking channels, you might get the impression that Cajun food uses seafood stock in everything, and that you throw everything left-over from cleaning seafood into a pot to make seafood stock: Fish heads, fins, bones and various other mean and nasty things. What these folks are actually doing is combining (and often confusing) French cooking with Cajun cooking, which admittedly can actually happen in authentic Cajun preparations, depending upon how close to New Orleans you get. In southeastern Louisiana, the Creole influence often winds up in Cajun cuisine, leading to more tomato-based dishes, lighter rouxs, and even tomatoes in gumbo. By the time you get to New Orleans, you get a big dose of French cooking thrown into the mix, and even lighter rouxs emerge, at which point the Cajun influence starts to fade. By contrast, bayou Cajun cooking has very small hints of French and Creole cooking, but are otherwise quite distinct, with very dark rouxs and dishes that are more full-bodied, featuring simple ingredients prepared carefully.

When Mama did use a seafood stock, she had a simple way to produce a mild seafood stock that would not overpower the dish. She would make it when she prepared shrimp for a dish. In a stock pot, she would place shrimp shells and shrimp heads along with just enough water to cover everything well and a little salt. She would boil the shells and heads for about 30 to 40 minutes and then strain the liquid and discard the shells. Mama said that this type of stock tasted "cleaner" and did not take over the dish you were trying to prepare. She felt that there should be nothing in a recipe that did not enhance whatever the main item of the dish was, whether that be shrimp, crab, oysters or fish (which she called "da star of da show"). As previously mentioned, most of the time Mama used plain water in her seafood dishes, but you can substitute seafood stock for the water in most of the seafood recipes include in this book if you prefer. If you want to take a page out of Cora's playbook, try using chicken stock in some of the seafood gumbos you cook. It will make the gumbo a little heartier and will not detract from the seafood. Another Cora-ism was to use chicken stock instead of water when cooking rice, along with a cup of chopped green onions and minced parsley. Boudreaux and Theroit will be comin' down da bayou for this *riz*.

Cora's Cornbread

When I was very young, Mama always cooked cornbread in very big batches. This was done for several reasons, not the least of which was that we ate a lot of cornbread. She was also concerned about the cost of using the oven, and the fact that the oven heated up the house considerably (especially during the summer months). Money was always very tight when I was young, and the oven was a big energy consumer, so Mama always tried to bake as much as she could when "I got da oven hot," as she used to say. The fact that the oven heated up the house a lot was also probably why we ate more baked goods in the winter than in the brutal coastal summers. My childhood home, besides being meager, was not insulated (as was common in those days, especially for bayou Cajuns). As such, our house was cold in the winter, but Mama kept us all warm with love. Mama had a way of keeping your mind off of the things that bothered you. She also would devise ways for you to get warm during bed-time, when all of the butane gas heaters would be turned off and the house would start getting cold very quickly. There were always stories circulating about some family being gassed in their sleep, or a house burning down because of faulty heaters. Gas-fired heaters had ceramic inserts that heated up and radiated out a lot of heat, especially if you were standing right in front of them. Since the bed was always very cold when you first got in, Mama would make us heat ourselves up real good; then she would heat up one of the many quilts that she had made. She would tell us to run quick and get into the bed, and she would run behind us and put the hot quilt directly over us. She would then pull the cold covers up over the quilt so that you were warm as toast, but only for a short while. Looking back, I now see that what made me feel so warm was not really the heated quilt, but actually

Mama hugging me for a while after she had covered me with it. Mama would then go about the task of shutting down the house for the night. When I would ask if she was cold, she would reply, "Oh *chere*, Mamas and Daddies don't get cold."

Mama and Daddy both got up at anywhere between two and four o'clock depending upon the season of the seafood that we were pursuing, and Mama would often warm the house by baking something like biscuits and cornbread. Leftover cornbread was never a problem since us kids (and Daddy) all liked Mama's cornbread dressing so much. To make the cornbread, she would first light the oven and bring it up to about 400 deg. F. Cornbread needs to be cooked in a hot oven, and Mama used to say that her oven cooked hotter than usual, so that is how she arrived at 400 deg. While the oven was warming, she would place two large, cast-iron skillets in the oven to heat up. Then while the oven and skillets were getting hot, she would make her cornbread. Mama always started with her dry ingredients first, carefully blending 4 cups of *farine de maïs* (pronounced *fah rin' may*, meaning corn meal) with 4 cups of whole wheat flour, ⅓ cup of baking powder, 2 teaspoons of salt, and about ⅓ cup of sugar. In a separate bowl she would blend her wet ingredients, which were 4 cups of milk, 1 cup of vegetable oil and four slightly beaten eggs. When she had buttermilk, she would substitute it for whole milk, but she said you had to add baking soda to make the butter milk work. After blending the wet and dry ingredients together to form a very thick batter, she would remove the hot cast iron skillets from the oven and pour about ¼ cup vegetable oil into each of them, and then tilt them around until all of the bottom and sides were well-oiled. Then she would pour about ½ of the corn bread batter into each skillet and put them back into the heated oven for about 25 to 30 minutes until a toothpick came out dry. I remember her flattening out the center of the batter in each skillet with her large mixing spoon so that it would come out more uniform instead of being very thick in the middle and thin on the sides. When we would say how good the cornbread was, Mama would tell us it was because she used whole wheat flour instead of white flour. Her cornbread had a nutty goodness that I still remember to this day.

Good cornbread is not hard to make, but it does take some attention to a few detail that make it really outstanding. If you use the following recipe, you should get very good results.

Cora's Corn Bread

INGREDIENTS:

2 cups	Corn Meal (stone ground if you can find it)
2 cups	Whole wheat flour
1 tsp.	Salt
3 tbsp.	Baking powder
4 tbsp.	Sugar
2	Eggs (slightly beaten)
2 cups	Whole milk
½ cup	Vegetable oil

Pre-heat your oven to a very hot 400 deg. to 450 deg. F, depending upon how your oven cooks. If you have found your oven cooks "hotter" or "colder," then adjust accordingly. Since modern ovens are pretty well-controlled, 425 deg. F would probably suffice until experience tells you otherwise. Place a medium sized cast-iron skillet into the oven while it is pre-heating.

Completely blend all of your dry ingredients in a large mixing bowl and then make a "well" in the middle of the dry mix. Gently pour in milk, beaten eggs and oil. Stir the wet ingredients in the well you have made in the dry mix until slightly combined, then thoroughly mix all ingredients until you get a very thick batter.

Once the cast iron skillet is completely heated, remove it from the oven and pour in ¼ cup of vegetable oil, tilting the skillet until the bottom and side of the skillet are completely coated. Then pour in your batter and stir with your mixing spoon in a circular pattern to flatten out your batter so the center will not be too thick.

Bake for about ½ hour or a little less until a toothpick inserted into the center comes out dry. Cut in pieces and serve while hot with lots of butter.

Variations on this recipe are numerous. Mama used to cut up shrimp or crawfish with chilies and yellow onions, sauté them in a pan and then add them to the recipe, along with a can of cream style corn. The favorite variation was when Mama sautéed chopped up yellow onions with crab meat and green onions, which she added to the corn meal batter before she baked it. I can still remember that glorious smell.

But wait: These variations are getting very close to Mama's cornbread dressing, which she made relatively often. Mama made cornbread dressing with any leftover cornbread, regardless of what variation she had cooked. In addition to being the master of maximum utilization and economy that she was, Cora's position was that cornbread dressing had endless possibilities, and all of them were good. I can still see her standing over her little stove where she would sauté each vegetable that she was going to put in the dressing until it was just right. She always used yellow onions, celery, green bell peppers, fresh parsley and green onions, but she would occasionally add colored bell peppers and sometimes broccoli when some were growing in the garden. She also liked to put some chopped nuts in her dressing, especially walnuts, but she mostly would use pecans which she had on hand more often. Sometimes her dressing had leftover chicken or turkey chopped up in it, especially around Thanksgiving or Christmas, which is always a special time for bayou Cajuns. When we had oysters, they were often put in her dressing; as were shrimp and crawfish. Mama's cornbread dressing was always delicious, and it always seemed to be a little different every time she made it.

You can make cornbread dressing that is customized to your tastes by adjusting the different elements of the recipe. One of the greatest things about cornbread dressing is that it is best made with leftover cornbread that had dried out somewhat. You therefore can cook the cornbread a day or two before you intend to serve it, thus completing a large part of the cooking prior to the day you intend to serve it.

The following ingredients are for a dressing made with the amount of cornbread that would be made from the previous recipe; however, it can be adjusted up or down depending upon how much cornbread with which you have to work. You almost cannot get it wrong since the elements of dressing are really very broad and encompassing. After you make corn bread dressing several times, you will be well aware of how you want to make it in the future.

Cornbread Dressing

INGREDIENTS:

2	Medium yellow onions
4 to 6	Ribs of celery
1	Large green bell pepper
1	Large red pepper
1 cup	Chopped green onions
¼ cup	Chopped fresh parsley
1 cup	Chopped walnuts or pecans
1 can	Chicken or vegetable stock
	Sufficient vegetable oil to sauté' each vegetable

Options:

½ lb.	Shrimp, crawfish or crabmeat (or some combination of each)
1 pint	Oysters
	Sufficient butter to sauté' each seafood
1 cup	Chopped left-over chicken or turkey

Into a large mixing bowl or deep stock pot, crumble up all of the corn bread into small pieces but not too fine. Sauté each vegetable (except the green onions and parsley) until it is cooked either soft or crunchy depending on your preference, but remember that they will be cooked a little more in the oven. As each of the vegetables is sautéed, add it to the crumbled corn bread. If using seafood, sauté it next and add to the corn bread; if not, add the cooked chicken or turkey, and stir until combined with the crumbled cornbread, then adding in the stock. The stock can be adjusted up or down for the correct amount of "wetness" of the mixture. The dressing should be sufficiently wet enough that it can be packed into a deep baking pan or dish that has been sprayed with cooking spray (I like olive oil). Bake in a 350 deg. F oven until it starts to form a slight crust – usually about 30 minutes. Cooking time is not critical since all of the ingredients are cooked already. I like to cut the dressing into squares and serve it with gumbo ladled over the squares, preferably made with the same type of seafood or chicken that was used in the dressing. *Si bon.*

Smother-Fried Turnips

I don't know if "smother frying" was invented by Cajuns, but if not they certainly have adopted and perfected it to some degree. My mother had a way of cooking vegetables that made them acceptable, possibly even enticing, for a somewhat reticent child. Turnips, for instance, are not exactly something that the average child would wish to have in their food pyramid; however, Cora had a way of cooking even turnips that made them not bad. Maybe even good, and as I got older, maybe even great.

Cora would begin by taking about 12 to 15 small to medium turnips and cutting off the tops and bottoms, and then thoroughly brushing them with a stiff vegetable brush. She would cut off any blemishes, but would not peel the turnips since she said that "all the flavor was in da skin". The turnips were then quartered or cut into approximately uniform pieces for even cooking, and some of the good leaves in the tops were washed and chopped for adding later. She would begin the cooking process by cutting up about four strips of bacon into about one-inch pieces and frying them in a large skillet over medium heat just until they were approaching crispy stage. Her position was that cooking the bacon until it was almost fully cooked developed the flavor more. She would then add a large, diced yellow onion and sauté over medium-high heat until the onion was starting to turn clear on the edges. The turnips were added and stirred for a couple of minutes to slightly brown the edges, and then about a cup of water was added to deglaze the pan and make what Cora called "short gravy." After stirring until most of the stuck-on bits were floating in the short gravy, the pot was covered and the heat was lowered to simmer the dish until the pieces were done to the desired tenderness when pierced with a fork. During cooking, a small amount of water might need to be added to maintain the same amount of short gravy, but not too much. Top with some finely-chopped green onions and serve. What you end up with is a bayou Cajun vegetable dish that I cook and eat until this day.

If you find this recipe a bit earthy for your taste, try some of these enhancements that were possibly provoked by leaving the bayou and going to college. In place of the regular bacon, I sometimes like to use thick-sliced, apple wood smoked bacon, which I'm sure would make my cardiologist excited. I also like to substitute a cup (or more) of white Zinfandel (or any other medium-dry wine that you might have) in place of the water. I have found that the sharpness of the turnips can be somewhat balanced by adding some carrots along with the turnips. Additionally, the chopped greens might be a little overpowering for our city guests, so adjust the amount added down or delete them if greens are not your thing. The bacon usually adds enough salt for my taste but you might want to salt to taste.

INGREDIENTS:

4	Strips of bacon
10-12	Small to medium turnips (and some carrots if desired)
1	Large yellow onion
½ cup	Chopped green onions
1 cup	Water (or wine)

CHAPTER SEVEN

COOKING WITH MAMA

Cooking with Cora

I was Cora's chief assistant in the kitchen. Cora loved to cook and she passed that love of cooking for loved ones down to me. When anyone came to our house, they all ended up in the kitchen talking to Mama while she cooked for them. Cora cooked so effortlessly that it almost did not seem like she was doing very much. On the contrary, she was doing quite a lot; she simply did not have a wealth of cooking devices to make the work of cooking easier. She made up for this with energy, which she possessed in great quantities.

During my early life, our home was in the marshes of a small fishing village at the Texas/Louisiana border on the coast of the Gulf of Mexico. Our nearest neighbor was a pretty good distance (or at least further than I was allowed to go), so I did not have friends to play with during this time. I had three older sisters who were not much interested in spending any time with me, so I was left to spend much of my time with Mama. This meant that I spent a lot of time in the kitchen helping Mama with cooking and canning.

To my mother, cooking was an art that involved precise execution. Her cooking philosophy was centered on the item being cooked, and not a profusion of spices and other ingredients. She believed in simple dishes that highlighted the subject of the cooking, allowing it to really shine. Mama always said that the main flavor that you want to taste in a given dish is the main ingredient. Any seasoning or spice that you introduce, then, should be subtle and only be used to enhance or nudge the flavor of the main ingredient along. The other side of the coin, however, is that the cooking process becomes much more important with this approach. Cora believed that all items used had to be cut and prepared precisely, and that the heat of preparation and timing of the introduction of all elements of the dish where the things that made a culinary creation something to behold. Mama's boundless energy level and her attention to detail made her cooking creations real showstoppers. Everybody wanted to eat at Cora's.

Cora's Crab and Shrimp Omelets

The most memorable breakfasts I have had in my life came from my Mama, and they occurred not in the comfort of home but in between "drags" (the time interval for pulling or dragging the shrimp trawl before it is pulled in, emptied, and returned to the water again) on Cotton's shrimp boat. By the time Cotton got me up in the wee hours of the morning to go out on the shrimp boat, he and Mama had been up for a while. I would awaken to the buttery smell of yellow onions being sautéed in Mama's iron skillet in preparation for the creation of a crab omelet, or a shrimp omelet, or a combination of both. When the onions were slightly clear, Mama would put two or three pounds of crab meat in the skillet, and sometimes some small peeled boiled shrimp, add more butter and continue until the crab meat (which was already cooked) was heated and incorporated with the butter and onions. Then she would pour 10 or 12 beaten eggs with a little whole milk and chopped green onions over the mixture, and stir gently until the eggs had completely set. She would then put a very generous layer of the omelet between two pieces of whole wheat bread and wrap the sandwich in waxed paper, then in foil while it was still hot. By the time we had taken the boat out and put the net in the water to begin the first "drag," the omelet sandwiches were still warm and oh-so-good. Mama always made Daddy and me several sandwiches because she said that men working needed plenty of food.

In retrospect, the rough setting of Cotton's shrimp boat with its worn equipment and even more worn finish, coupled with the smell and touch of the salty air, created a certain romance for which words are insufficient. The sea birds were talking to each other, as they continuously did while looming overhead. Such a setting was hardly the place you would expect for a dish as lofty as a crab meat omelet to be served. Yet, as I look back, it was the perfect place. The eye of the beholder was most probably influenced by the simplicity of the environment and of the times. The dominate factor in the entire experience was the love I could feel emanating from Mama. No matter what time Cotton decided to start his day, Cora would be up and ready for action. She assisted with preparations for the day's activities, and always provided something for us to eat that went well beyond that which would be considered sufficient.

When you eat this dish, the biggest surprise is its simplicity. It is basically a few very outstanding ingredients combined at the right time and circumstances to become something really great. You can scale this recipe up or down to suit the number of guests or size of appetites, but it is very rich to the taste so, something to accompany it (perhaps some fruit) would probably work nicely.

Cora's Crab Omelet

INGREDIENTS:

1 lb. Blue crab meat (other species of crab meat will work)
1 stick Butter
6 Eggs (beaten)
1 Small to med. yellow onion (chopped finely)
1 cup Chopped green onion tops
1 tbsp. Lemon juice
¼ cup Whole milk

In a cast iron skillet, sauté yellow onion in one to two tablespoons of the butter until slightly clear, then melt the remainder of the butter and incorporate the crab meat and lemon juice, stirring gently so not to break up the crab meat too much. Since the crab meat is already cooked, you are simply warming it up and combining it with the melted butter. If you are using raw crab meat, add three to five minutes to sauté time. Combine the beaten eggs, milk and green onions, and add those into the skillet, again stirring gently until the eggs have set and cooked to your taste. Serve with French bread that has been sliced open, buttered and toasted under a broiler.

This same recipe can be altered to include small boiled shrimp or raw shrimp as the case may be. The only change here would be to sauté the raw shrimp with the onions initially to cook the shrimp. The shrimp can be substituted directly for the crab meat, or you can use half and half with the crab meat. Either way, you are in for an exquisite treat.

Cora's *Pacane* Pie

Mama must have really liked pecans, because her best desserts all seemed to prominently feature them. Mama's *pacane* (pronounced *pa con'*) pie was a standout from the others I have eaten; mostly, I think, because it had more pecans in it, and it was a deeper dish variety. Mama had a deep dish, 10 inch pie pan that she liked to use, so the ingredients need to be altered somewhat for a 9 inch (deep dish) pie crust because I expect that some of you attempting this recipe are going to go to your local gleaming big-box to purchase a sweat-shop, stamped-out pie crust in a disposable foil pan. It will still taste good, but you just won't be able to hear the accordion music in the distance as you eat your still-warm pie. For a 9 inch pan, use ½ cup each of brown sugar and melted butter, one less egg and ½ cup less pecans.

FILLING INGREDIENTS:

4	Eggs
½ tsp.	Salt
⅓ cup	Melted butter
1 tbsp.	Corn starch
1 tbsp.	White flour
1 tsp.	Pure vanilla extract
⅔ cup	Brown sugar
1 ½ cups	Pure cane syrup
1 ½ cups	Pecans chopped (roughly)
	Pecan halves

For those of you who want to make the pie crust, Mama's recipe for pie crust follows. If, however, you grabbed an insta-crust at the Super Zip-Zap Mart (you know, the one with the yuppie coffee shop inside), you should pierce it at several points with a fork before adding in the pie mixture.

Melt butter and then combine with flour and cornstarch, and stir until thoroughly mixed. Then add in sugar, cane syrup and salt and bring to a gentle boil, and maintain that boil for about 2 to 3 minutes. Place pan in a basin of cool water until mixture is cooled, and then add in the beaten eggs, chopped pecans and vanilla blending well. A word of caution - make certain the mixture is cooled down sufficiently before you add in the eggs, or you will have scrambled eggs in your pecan pie. Pour the mixture into your prepared pie crust and place the pecan halves on top of the mixture. Bake on a pre-heated cookie sheet in a hot oven at 425 deg. F for about 10 minutes, then reduce heat to 350 deg. F oven for about 30 to 40 minutes. If the edges of the pie crust start to brown too soon, cut strips of foil and cover them. Mama always said that you could lightly tap the center of the pie and it should spring back if it is sufficiently done.

Pecane

Remove from oven and completely cool so that the filling will "set."

As kids, we never could wait for it to fully set because we wanted to eat it while it was still warm. If you feel the same impulse, then you have to serve it in bowls and eat it with a spoon (and alongside some of Cora's homemade vanilla ice cream, but that's another recipe).

The "if you really want to impress your mother-in-law" version: Occasionally, Mama would make a different version of this pie by adding about 4 ounces of unsweetened chocolate into the mixture, along with about a ½ cup of bourbon whiskey. If you choose to try this, you need to do the following:

On very low heat, melt butter and chocolate in a saucepan until completely blended, then combine with all of the other ingredients (including the whiskey) except the beaten eggs, vanilla and pecans. The other ingredients, when mixed in, will cool the mixture down somewhat then you blend in the eggs, vanilla and coat the pecans and precede the same as you did in the above steps. Again, a word of caution about making certain the mixture is cooled down sufficiently before you add in the eggs.

Mama's Pie Crust

So, you want the full effect, the big Cajun banana: You want to make your own crust. Luckily, making your own crust is not really that hard. The biggest thing to remember is that all of the ingredients need to be kept cold for best results. Mama had two different crusts that she made; the only difference was the type of fat used. One used butter, in which case keeping the ingredients cold was important, and the other was shortening (hydrogenated vegetable oil). There was nothing scaring the daylights out of us about "trans fats" when I was growing up, and Mama said that a pie crust made with shortening was always the best, and I tend to agree with her. Actually, at the time, there were more health fears attached to using butter, but now butter has become the lessor of two (or more) evils. Regardless, shortening is a natural for pie crust and is much easier to work with, but the trans fats thing makes it your choice. I ate a lot of them growing up, and I am still here. The fact that I may look like a "train wreck" is certainly not wholly attributable to shortening pie crusts when you consider all of the other Cajun foods I have consumed in vast quantities.

Well, here it is, with butter. If you want to use shortening, then just substitute it for the butter in the same quantities and you don't have to put it in the refrigerator between the mixing and rolling out stages.

INGREDIENTS:

2 cups   All-purpose flour
2/3 cup   Butter
6 tbsp.   Ice water
A pinch of salt

In a mixing bowl, combine the flour and salt and then "cut in" the butter with a pastry cutter. Begin adding the water as you are cutting in the butter until all of the water is added and the ingredients resemble a coarse crumbly mixture. Form into a ball and wrap in waxed paper and put into the fridge for at least ½ hour. Handling and manipulating the dough causes heat so you refrigerate it to keep the butter from melting prior to baking.

Next, you remove the dough ball from the frig and roll it out to the desired thickness, using only enough flour to keep it from sticking. Too much added flour at this point will make the dough less flakey. Place the crust in a pie pan and cut and form a decorative edge (if desired). Pierce the crust thoroughly with a fork to prevent the crust from developing an air bubble during baking.

If you are not ready for the crust right away, then put it in the frig to keep it cold until you are ready for use. You a real Cajun now, *chere*.

Cora's Pecan Pralines

Although Mama didn't make many dishes in the dessert category, she did have a few notable standouts. I do have to say, as a pecan lover, that Mama's pecan pralines were some of the best I have ever tasted. Mama alternated between dark and light brown sugar when making this recipe – I think it was more dependent upon what she had on hand, but the dark brown sugar recipe reminds me most of my childhood. Heed the warning! These pralines are definitely habit-forming.

INGREDIENTS:

5 cups   Brown sugar
6 tbsp.   Water
1 tbsp.   Butter
2 cups   Whole pecans
Several drops of pure vanilla extract *(sometimes when Mama was feeling adventurous, she would use coconut extract)*
Waxed paper, cut in about 6 inch squares

Simmer the brown sugar and water in a saucepan, stirring constantly, until the syrup will thread. You then remove the syrup from heat and stir in butter until melted then stir in vanilla and pecans until fully coated. On each sheet of waxed paper, drop a large spoonful of the pecan mixture. Let stand until cooled and the mixture sets. If you close your eyes while you are eating these you should be able to hear "Jole Blon" (possibly the Cajun national anthem) played on a Cajun accordion. If you don't then you either did not try this while the pralines were still a little warm or you did not get the recipe right and you need to start over.

One final note of caution, if you consume more than four of these in less than a five minute period, you should not operate equipment or machinery because, at that point, you will probably be saturated with euphoria.

Mama's Beignets

The *beignet* (pronounced *ben yay* and meaning "bump" in French, probably because of the rather over-puffed appearance of this fried fritter) is commonly associated with a historic coffee shop in the French quarter of New Orleans. Beignets were brought to the new world by the *Acadiens* when they resettled in the Louisiana area following the Great Upheaval and they have been somewhat of a common fixture of Cajun life since that time. So important are beignets that they became the official Louisiana state donut in 1986.

Mama's beignets were always a real treat for us since we seldom had "store-bought" items of that nature. Always served while hot, beignets are a fried, sugar-coated pastry that were always greeted by us with delight and it did not take too much urging by us to get Mama to make them. Probably due to her New Orleans roots, Cora always made her beignets accompanied by strong coffee (with chicory) *au lait* (pronounced *o lay*' and meaning with milk). Mama would heat up the milk and Daddy would brew some special coffee that was so strong you would have to drink it with half milk although Daddy still drank his black in a *demitasse* (pronounced *dim a tas* and meaning a half cup or half-sized cup in French).

Here is Mama's recipe for beignets which I have made many times to the delight of my children. My New Orleans born wife has pointed out to me that the dough in Mama's beignets is a little on the sweet side of authentic French Quarter beignets to which she is accustomed and that is probably accurate. Mama was probably a little heavy handed with sugar when she made her pastries and breads but I am sure she would tell you *"chere,* you got to mak it yur way..." If authenticity is what you desire, then you probably need to add a little more salt and a little less sugar to Mama's recipe and over time, you will get the taste that works best for you and your family.

INGREDIENTS:

3 cups	All-purpose flour
1 pkg.	Active dry yeast
½ cup	Warm water (+/- 100°F)
½ cup	Evaporated milk
½ cup	Sugar
¼ tsp.	Salt
2 Tbs.	Melted butter
1	Egg (beaten)

Activate the yeast by placing the contents of the package into the ½ cup of warm water with about a spoon full of sugar (from the ½ cup of sugar). Set aside for a few minutes.

Combine all the dry ingredients: flour, salt and sugar in a large mixing bowl, stirring well until completely mixed. In another bowl, combine egg, evaporated milk, butter and the activated yeast mixture, and stir until completely mixed. When all wet ingredients are mixed, stir into the dry ingredients and blend until a sticky dough is formed. You might need to mix with your hands to achieve this stage. If you have a strong mixer with a dough hook attachment, then this will be much easier.

Once dough ball is formed, place in a lightly greased bowl, cover with a clean towel and place bowl in a warm location to rise for about one to two hours until double in size. Once dough has risen, pour dough out onto a lightly floured surface and roll out until dough is about 1/8 inch thick and cut into 2 to 3 inch squares (or parallelograms) or whatever shape you like. Shape is not important as long as they are not too big.

Fry dough pieces in enough vegetable oil to float them at about 350°F to 360°F until lightly browned, turning for even cooking. This happens rather quickly so be ready. Using a slotted utensil, remove the beignets from the hot oil directly into a bowl with powdered sugar and toss to coat evenly. Serve hot with strong French roast coffee. *C'est si bon!*

CHAPTER EIGHT

ODE TO ROUX

"Hail, Muse... et cetera."
– Lord Byron

Ode to Roux

What can one say about roux? Currently, it seems that every television cooking personality touts his/her/their method of making roux as the most authentic ever made. Roux, however, is many things to many different people. To a French chef, it is the initial step in making a béchamel sauce. Many European nationalities use some form of roux (under different names) in the preparation of their ethnic dishes. To say that it merely is a cooking mixture of flour (wheat) and some type of oil is rather simplistic, especially when taken in the context of Cajun culture. To a Cajun, roux is the elixir of life or the *coup de grace* (pronounced *coo' day grah* and meaning a finishing stroke or blow). Almost every dish that I talked to my mother about starts off with "well, yoo make da roux …" (or maybe it just seems thusly with my Cajun bent). To a Cajun, roux is the ultimate deal-breaker. When I enter a house where any one of the forms of Cajun gumbos or stews is being prepared, I can usually tell by the smell permeating the air as to whether the roux was cooked to what I call the proper amount of darkness. It seems that my lifetime of interaction has led me to the conclusion that the darkness of the roux is different for every Cajun.

A roux is made by cooking (browning) flour in some type of oil. In French (haute) cuisine, the roux is most notably a thickening agent and is usually very light in color, being cooked for a short period and imparting very little flavor but a characteristic richness. To increase the richness, the oil employed is often butter. Many Creole dishes are derived from French cooking and use similar approaches to roux preparation. Cajun cooking, on the other hand, uses the nutty flavor of darker roux as a flavoring agent more than a thickener since roux becomes less effective at thickening as it gets darker. Vegetable oil is the fat of preference for Cajuns since it has a higher smoke point than butter for the time and heat durations needed to prepare dark roux.

How dark is dark roux? The best answer I have been able to discern is that as you travel east of Lafayette, Louisiana, the roux gets lighter and as you travel west, the roux gets darker. Lafayette is located in central Louisiana and seems to be the disputed capitol of the Cajun world (again, depending on which Cajun you talk to). The Creole influence is very strong towards the New Orleans area, hence the lighter rouxs and French influence. Southwestern Louisiana and the easternmost tip of Texas (where it meets the Gulf of Mexico) is the area of the bayou Cajuns and very dark roux.

The darker the roux, the more intense and lingering the aroma. Of course, to me, my mother made the very best dark roux. I can still remember that smell as I entered the house after a long day on the shrimp boat, and every time I make a roux, that aroma reminds me of Mama. The roux has to be just right for the final gumbo, ettouffe or stew to come out right.

In addition to the darkness of roux being an issue in Cajun cooking, the amount of roux used in a dish is a determinate factor. When a dish starts out "take two tablespoons of flour in 1/4 cup of oil and make a roux" you ain't talking about making something that a bayou Cajun is going to eat unless you are only making one cup of gumbo. The recipes I have included talk in terms of pints and quarts of roux. The major difference between what my Mama called a gumbo and a stew was actually twice the amount of roux used. A stew also has a somewhat higher seafood to liquid ratio, but the amount of roux is the principle difference.

What if there were no Green Onions?

The lowly green onion, *allium schoenoprasum*, also referred to as "spring onions," has a special place in my heart. It was one of my Mama's favorite ingredients, and it renders a flavor that defines bayou Cajun food to me. Mama always had an old washtub (or three) that had been repurposed as a living storehouse for her supply of green onions. Since we were in the seafood business, we always had an old no. 3 washtub that had outlived its usefulness for holding shrimp. It was Mama's working theory that green onions had to be cut fresh and added to whatever dish she was using them in at precisely the proper time to impart the flavor she was trying to achieve. I cannot imagine eating one of her crabmeat omelets, shrimp and crab gumbo, or especially her stuffed crabs without the distinct taste provided by green onions tops. To this day, when I make cornbread dressing the way Mama taught me, I have to have fresh grown, green onion tops or it is just not the same.

Like Mama, I keep green onions growing in the edge of any garden that I have. Anyone can start their own green onion garden by simply buying a bunch or two of fresh green onions at the market and cutting off about one inch of the bottom of each green onion, and then pushing it about one inch deep in the dirt and about one inch apart, at the edge of any garden around the house (it does not have to be a vegetable garden). You can even plant your cut onion bottoms in any type pot with a drainage hole in the bottom, as long as you use plenty of compost mixed in with the dirt and remember to water regularly. Even you city folks living in those "bird houses" (apartment dwellers) can buy composted manure and mix it with potting soil in a flower pot to grow green onions out on your patio. You will be pleasantly surprised at how quickly the green tops will begin to appear, and within a couple of weeks you can begin harvesting the tops for use in the kitchen. Every time you cut the tops off, within a couple of weeks you can cut them again. After about six to eight months, the bottoms will get too big to produce the smaller, more tasty tops, and you can then pull them all up and buy several bunches at the market to start over. Don't forget to add more compost when you re-plant, and to use the big bottoms and tops you pulled up in making you next vegetable stock. Anyone can have a constant supply of very fresh green onions with the smallest amount of effort.

When green onions are added to a dish, they undergo a change which makes the timing of their addition somewhat critical if you want the precise taste they provide. Only a small exposure to heat is needed to "flash off" the stronger taste that overrides the smoother flavor that green onions give a dish. Very quickly, green onions can overcook, and any flavor they might have added will disappear completely. Because of this, Mama was very careful in this regard and would actually allow soups and stews to cool down a little before adding the chopped green onion tops, or would add the chopped green onions to a bowl before adding in the hot liquid to minimize such flavor losses. Because baked dishes such as dressings are cooked somewhat more gently, extra care is not needed, and the green onions are added to the stuffing prior to baking. I can still remember sitting down to a large bowl of rice that Mama had dusted with freshly ground file' and sprinkled with chopped green onion tops, and then that heavenly smell when she ladled on the hot shrimp and crab gumbo. "*Lessez les bons temps rouler*" (pronounced *lazay lay bon tawn roolay* and means "let the good times roll").

CHAPTER NINE

Roux, Bayou Cajun Style

"Furst, yoo make da roo."
– Cora LaBove

Roux, Bayou Cajun Style

You will probably be surprised to find that the making of what appears to be a simple browning of flour in oil is significantly complicated by the skill needed to get the finished roux dark enough. At the risk of getting into the dark roux/light roux controversy, let us just accept the fact that for bayou Cajuns recipes, the roux must always be very dark.

The best roux is made in a seasoned cast iron pot. Aside from the fact that cast iron cookware was durable and affordable (and thus the cookware of choice for bayou Cajuns), it also holds residual heat very well, and does not change temperature very quickly, which is a good thing when making roux. Mama had a large cast iron skillet that she called her roux pot, and she did not use it for anything else. It made a little less than three quarts of roux when you made as much roux as you dared. Because roux keeps very well, Mama always made a full skillet, and she would keep it in quart jars in the ice box. Cajuns still call their refrigerator an "ice box" because they were probably the last American ethnic group to get electricity, and prior to that time actually did have a box for holding food in which they

An old-time "ice box"

would put a block of ice. I inherited Mama's roux pot and most of her other cast iron dutch ovens, stock pots and skillets, and I treasure them.

Making roux is somewhat like a cat walking along the top edge of a wooden fence; you are only one small step away from disaster at any moment. The very residual heat that your cast iron "roux pot" has been providing as a good thing can instantly turn into a bad thing if you happen to get the heat too high for a minute. Your roux pot then turns into the enemy, and you only have one small measure of control to prevent the roux from burning, and that is vigorously stirring (with a wooden spoon) or as my dad said "yoo gotta stir like hell chere". Mama did not use a wooden spoon per se; it was actually more like a flattened wooden spatula with rounded corners that my dad made for her. She said it got into the corners of the pot better than a wooden spoon, so she did not miss stirring any part of the roux. The creation of roux could actually be referred to as a "controlled burn." When Mama was teaching me to make roux, she said "yoo gotta burn it jus rite". If, during the process of making roux, you ever see dark flecks appear in the mixture, you would just as well throw it away, because it will destroy any dish in which you use it. After you have invested about a half hour of constant stirring and anguish, and it feels like your arm is about to fall off but you dare not stop stirring, the decision to throw it all away and start over is not an easy one. You must remember that the time you exhaust and the money you spend for seafood is too large an investment to have it all be unsatisfactory in the end, so if you burn your roux it is better to just "suck it up," throw it away, and start over.

Now you have your cast iron roux pot (a skillet works best for stirring), and it is seasoned, but that's another story in itself; and you have your wooden spoon or device your husband (or wife, as the case may be) made in their workshop; and you are finally ready to make roux. The recipe is simple – roughly equal parts of flour (Mama preferred unbleached) and vegetable oil combined in your roux pot as you are beginning to bring the temperature up – I usually start out on medium heat. When you are learning, it is best not to try to make too much roux at a time, because Mama said that when you are learning to make roux you have to burn it at least once to fully understand your perimeters (not her exact words). I would start out with a cup of each, and adjust the flour until you get a very thick batter consistency. Once everything is combined and very hot, I raise the temperature up a little to about medium high (depending upon your stove type), always remembering to never stop stirring. In addition to constant stirring, you have to develop a pattern where you manage to cover all of the bottom of the pot with some degree of regularity. If everything is going well, you will watch the mixture go from light tan, to brown, to dark brown, to about the shade of dark chocolate, and then you turn off the heat and you have made it.

But not so fast – you now have a mixture that is half oil, very hot, and you have about 30 seconds to figure out a way to stop the cooking – and don't forget, you can't stop stirring. Well, what I did not tell you so far was that before you start, you must arrange enough platters (high temperature type) so that you can pour out and spread your roux to about a one inch or less thickness to cool. That is, unless you intend to use all of the roux you have cooked, in which case you have a couple of chopped up onions to throw into the roux, and the water in the onions will cool off the roux sufficiently to stop the cooking process. As you are stirring the onions into the roux to cool it off, the aroma that you will be experiencing is the very essence of bayou Cajun life – the smell of my childhood – the Cajun version of mom and apple pie.

Well, after a description like the one I just outlined, I guess that you are now thoroughly afraid to attempt roux. Don't be – after a few successes and a few failures, you will be a pro. I can still remember Mama making roux. She would fill her large roux pot half full with oil and start adding in flour until she liked the consistency, all while she related stories to me about her childhood. The next thing I knew, there were three large platters of hot roux on the table cooling. This ritual was played about once (or twice) a week, which is why my sisters and I have all ended up taking statins.

If you want the Cajun experience, you have to successfully make roux at least once in your lifetime. Just try it – take the plunge. Then you can start using store-bought roux while bitchin' about how it's not as good as the roux you make. When you do that, then you are an honorary Cajun cause that's what all of the one's I know right now do.

The Butter Roux

There is a type of roux that Mama used to make which she reserved for special occasions when she wanted to make something really rich. It was what we called butter roux, because it was made with real butter and not vegetable oil. I only remember her using it in a handful of dishes, and I do not remember her making extra to keep in the refrigerator for later use. I suspect that it probably does not keep well because of the fact that it was made with butter, although I personally have never made enough extra to refrigerate and have on hand. On something as important as roux is to bayou Cajun cooking, I tend to emulate Cora's methodology without a lot of deviation. Mama, for whatever reason, did not make extra butter roux to refrigerate for later use, so I do not.

I do remember the difference that a butter-based roux makes in dishes like crawfish *étouffée* (pronounced *et too faye*) and crawfish bisque. I have eaten these dishes made with regular roux (vegetable oil base) and butter roux, and I can tell you that there is a definite difference. There is not much difference between the making of butter roux and its vegetable oil brethren. Butter has a lower burn point though, so it gets a bit tricky in the final stages of browning. I usually do not try to get it as dark brown as I do with vegetable oil; usually stopping at the milk chocolate appearance instead of the dark chocolate shade of vegetable roux. Other than that, all other procedures are pretty much the same. Butter roux requires about equal parts melted butter to flour; however, I find myself adjusting the mixture with flour to get the heavy batter viscosity that I am comfortable with (as I saw my Mama do countless times). All of the other cautions and procedures are about the same. As with vegetable oil based roux, at the precise moment it is done, cooling the roux down to avoid further cooking (burning) is very important. And again, lowering the heat by stirring in chopped onions will cool the roux down sufficiently, as will spooning it into heat resistant platters or pans to cool.

Do not be afraid to try and make butter roux. If you want to use it in any of your dishes, then you will have to make it yourself, since I do not know of any commercial source for butter based roux as of this printing. If you burn it past the point of use, then throw it out and start over. Once you master making butter roux, you will be glad you took the time to do so.

Gumbo

It has been said that if you cut a Cajun, he will bleed gumbo. Gumbo is the central dish of the Cajun culture, and it is served as the main dish (as well as being served as an accompanying dish) in many meals. Gumbo is a Cajun celebration food and considered a "must-have" for almost all social events and gatherings. Gumbo is also the official cuisine of the state of Louisiana.

Gumbo originated in southern Louisiana sometime in the 1700's. Gumbo could possibly have been based upon the French dish *bouillabaisse* (pronounced *boo' ya baze*) as well as traditional dishes from West Africa, or even an amalgamation of both elements. Two of the early ingredients for thickening gumbo; okra, a vegetable from Africa that was probably introduced into America by slaves; and *filé* (pronounced *fee' lay*), a spice made by the Choctaw Indians which was a powder made from the ground leaves of the sassafras tree, could possibly account for its name. The Choctaw Indian tribe was indigenous to the area that later became Louisiana. The Choctaw word for filé was *kombo*, and the African word for okra was *ki ngombo*, and both could have played some part in the derivation of the name for gumbo.

Gumbo is a stew-like dish that exists in several different varieties. It contains mostly poultry or game meats (but not pork and beef), as well as vegetables and available spices. It often is centered around seafood, but seafood is seldom used in combination with meat. A notable exception is one of my father's favorite dishes, chicken and oyster gumbo. While bayou Cajuns make gumbos which are characterized by very dark, heavy rouxs, and Creole Cajuns typically make gumbo with light colored rouxs, some Cajun cultures in other parts of the state make gumbo based more on filé, while others use tomatoes in their gumbo. Bayou Cajuns would never put tomatoes in their gumbo, however.

The Catholic religion is fairly prominent in the Cajun culture, and during Lent (when Catholics are expected to abstain from eating meat), the Cajuns found a way to continue eating gumbo. They created a meatless dish called *gumbo des herbes,* which translates into gumbo with herbs, and was later shortened to *gumbo z'herbes.* Gumbo z'herbes was a dish centered around mustard greens, spinach and turnips. Even though the derivation of gumbo z'herbes is probably linked to the German Catholic use of stews made with greens during the Lenten period, the Cajun culture most likely made gumbo z'herbes uniquely their own.

In the Cajun culture, gumbo is also a central feature in the celebration of Mardi Gras. In an event known as *courir de Mardi Gras,* local men would roam from house to house and beg for ingredients to make a gumbo. They would then gather at some central location and make a large gumbo. When the gumbo was ready, the group would eat gumbo and dance until midnight when Lent would begin. Gumbo was also served at Cajun dance parties known as *fais do-do*, where gumbo was usually served at midnight.

Gumbo is a dish that is unique to the Cajun culture. There are many versions of gumbo, and they all claim to be authentic. I cannot comment in that regard, but I do know that the origins of my family were the bayous and salt marshes of southeast Texas and southwestern Louisiana, and the recipes that I have compiled for you are what we were raised to believe is gumbo. We always make a large pot of gumbo since it improves in flavor every time you remove it from the refrigerator and re-warm it. We will intentionally eat all of the seafood or chicken from the gumbo and slowly bring it to a boil (gumbo burns on the bottom very easily so stir frequently when re-heating), add more mirepoix and more seafood or chicken, and then simmer for 20 to 45 minutes (depending on cooking time for added items); you are then ready to go again. I would not recommend keeping it refrigerated for over a week or so for food's safety sake, but ours has never seemed to last any longer than that anyway.

A Word About Gumbo Filé

Filé is a Cajun seasoning that is simply the dried and ground leaves of the sassafras tree. Sassafras trees are indigenous to areas of high rainfall and high humidity, and are important to the Cajun people for several uses, not the least of which is filé powder. The roots were boiled to make a tea that was used as medicine for colds and flu-like symptoms (since it acts as a diuretic). The oils extracted from the roots had antiseptic and analgesic properties, and were used in many Cajun home remedies. The berries produced by the tree were consumed by many of the animals hunted by Cajuns. The heartwood was used to smoke meats, and the bark was used for dyes. Cajuns always knew where there were sassafras trees growing.

What is Mirepoix

Mirepoix (pronounced *merr pwah*) is a French word that in traditional cooking circles refers to a combination of onions, celery and carrots which creates a flavor base for a wide variety of dishes. Similarly, the Spanish have *sofrito* (onions, garlic and tomatoes), the Portuguese have *soffritto* (onions, garlic and celery) and many other cultures have combinations that have their favorite vegetables as a flavor base. To the *Acadiens* (Cajuns), mirepoix is onions, celery and bell peppers, and the combination is also jokingly referred to as the "holy trinity." My only addition to the "trinity" would be to humbly add green onion, which is the ingredient that imparts the distinctive Cajun flavor in crab dishes, especially stuffed crabs and crab cakes. As mentioned, every bayou Cajun I know had an old washtub full of dirt with green onions growing near the back door next to their "bird's eye" pepper bush.

In the gumbo recipe, the mirepoix you add will totally cook away in the first half of the simmering time, creating a vegetable stock. For additional flavor enhancement, the same ingredients can be added again, especially if you like to have some cooked vegetables in your dish for improved texture and visual appeal. You are encouraged to experiment with additional mirepoix additions and elements to enhance your gumbo to taste.

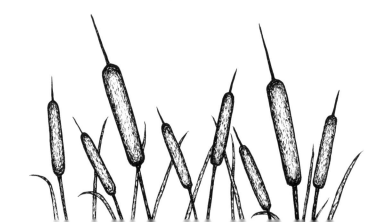

Cora's Shrimp & Crab Gumbo

When I was young, the smell of Mama cooking gumbo permeated the house with a high degree of frequency. Oh that glorious smell – I can close my eyes and smell it right now! The aroma of Mama's dark roux when she was making gumbo is the most vivid memory that I have of her. When I cook gumbo today, I can still imagine Mama stirring gumbo in her tiny kitchen, or in the work shed where Daddy had piped butane so that Mama could cook on a small two-burner cooker, or even in the yard over a wood fire. It did not matter what the circumstances, Mama could cook, oblivious to any difficulties that may have been present. But that was the way of bayou Cajuns – working and dealing with the difficult life that they had been assigned by fate's lottery. My Mama embraced the hard life with an eternal zest that belied any rigors that were present. Cora was almost always jovial, and was comfortable with who she was and with what she had. Mama knew that gumbo was one of me and my sisters' favorite dishes, and she was always happily willing to cook it for us.

Like seemingly all Cajuns, Cora was pretty opinionated about the manner in which her gumbo was cooked, and the combination of main ingredients for gumbo. Mama believed that the best gumbos were ones that featured no more than two main ingredients, i.e. shrimp and crab gumbo, chicken and oyster gumbo, goose gizzard and oyster gumbo, crawfish and crab gumbo, etc. She also did not like to add smoked sausage to her gumbos, since she felt that the smoked flavor "took over" the dish. She said many times that if you use sausage in gumbo, then you just as well make sausage gumbo. Since sausage seems to have become ubiquitous in most modern versions of gumbo that I have encountered, I will not broach that argument at this point; however, my opinion is in alignment with Cora's, and I still cook gumbo with two main ingredients and no sausage.

Chevrette (pronounced *shav rhett'*,
meaning shrimp) and crab gumbo
is probably my all-time favorite
combination for gumbo. Cora would
begin shrimp and crab gumbo by
bringing to a boil about four to five
quarts of water in a large stock pot

into which, she would dissolve about one pint of roux. Mama kept
roux she had made ahead in the refrigerator almost all of the time.
When the roux was totally dissolved, Cora would add the mirepoix
(see "Mirepoix"), and about 4 or 5 shrimp and two or three crabs.
After the gumbo had returned to a boil, she would lower the heat
to simmer for an hour or so, stirring occasionally. She always added
a small portion of whatever the featured ingredients were to "cook
away and flavor" the stock or base of the gumbo at the beginning of
cooking.

By this time, the mirepoix, shrimp and crabs (except for the
shells) had totally dissolved for the most part, and the broth was
thick and rich. At this point, Mama said that the base for the gumbo
was complete and now it was time to "make da gumbo good to eat."
Cora would then raise the heat and add minced *ail* (pronounced *aye*,
meaning garlic) and more mirepiox, since we all liked to have some
cooked vegetables present in the dish along with the crabs, as they
took a little longer to cook than the shrimp. After the gumbo had
returned to a boil, Cora would lower the heat for what she called "a
gentle boil." After the crabs had cooked for a few minutes, she would
add the shrimp, again raising the heat a little to return to boil, then
lowering the heat for a gentle boil. She would then carefully break an

egg into a cup and gently pour the egg down along the side of the pot in to the gumbo. She would slowly repeat this until there were about a dozen eggs in the gumbo. The eggs, though somewhat odd shaped, would pretty well stay together until they cooked. Although eating boiled eggs with gumbo might seem rather odd, the combination is quite flavorful and very representative of bayou Cajuns. When the eggs were boiled and the shrimp were done, she would turn the heat off and then stir in a cup or so of chopped green onions. The gumbo was finished.

To serve, Cora would put a generous helping of sticky white rice in a large bowl. She would then dust the rice with filé and top it with a few chopped green onions. To this bowl, Mama would add large ladles of shrimp, crabs and gumbo, along with two of the boiled eggs.

Returning from the days of yesteryear, I have attached a recipe that is based upon (and tastes reminiscent of) Mama's shrimp and crab gumbo; however, it is a little easier to perform and uses some enhancements I have found attractive. As you cook this gumbo, be ever-vigilant for changes that you can make for your own taste; after all, gumbo is a dish that developed from meager means, and is constantly evolving to this day. Any good Cajun will tell you that you must keep making gumbo with small alterations to "make it your own," and only then will you truly appreciate what gumbo is and was to the Cajun people.

Cora's Shrimp and Crab Gumbo

INGREDIENTS:

1	Pint of Roux
5	Quarts of water

The Mirepoix:

3	Large yellow onions
4	Cups of coarsely chopped celery
2	Large coarsely chopped green bell pepper
2 3 tbsps.	Vegetable oil
3 lbs.	Small to medium peeled shrimp
1 dozen	Cleaned blue crabs with claws separated *(or 4 cleaned Dungeness Crabs – each cut in half w/claws separated)*
1 cup	Chopped green onions
½ cup	Fresh chopped parsley
1 clove	Minced garlic
	One dozen eggs
5 tsps.	Sea salt (or to taste)
	Filé to taste

Optional:

2 to 4	Chopped jalapenos *(not exactly Cajun but tasty)*, or:
1-2 tsps.	Cayenne pepper *(very Cajun)*

Coarsely chop 2 of your 3 large yellow onions (reserve one onion for later), and combine with vegetable oil, celery, garlic, and bell pepper along with your choice of peppers (if desired) in a large stockpot over medium-high heat for a light sauté. Add water and bring to a rolling boil. Remove metal lid from the jar of roux and microwave for about 2 to 3 minutes until roux is warmed (warming the roux makes it melt and combine with the water quicker). Spoon roux into the boiling water, stirring continuously until all of the roux is completely melted. If excess foaming occurs that cannot be controlled by continuously stirring, lower heat and continue until all roux is dissolved. Lower heat and simmer for about one hour, stirring occasionally. At this point of the simmering process, a few shrimp and one crab body should be added in to flavor the liquid.

Boil one dozen eggs in a sauce pan until hard boiled. Crack and peel eggs, and reserve for later use when serving gumbo.

After simmering, crabs, claws and shrimp should be added to the mixture, and the heat should be elevated to return the mixture to a boil. The yellow onion that was reserved should be cut up in slices, separated into rings and dropped into the mixture for appearance and texture. You can additionally add a chopped red, yellow or orange bell pepper at this point. Lower heat to maintain low boil (and to cook seafood) for 20 to 30 minutes. Then, turn off heat and add parsley and green onions. Serve over cooked rice with filé and one or two peeled, hard boiled eggs.

Cora's Chicken and Dumplins

Mama's Chicken & Dumplins (dumplings) were not the garden variety so commonly eaten in many parts of the country today. They were definitely hearty and filling, and the Cajun touch was obvious from the first bite. I grew up on this style of chicken and dumplings, so it is probably unfair to judge all recipes by this standard, especially since Cajuns seem to eat everything with some greater or lesser amount of roux added. The inherent richness of any gravy that has been enhanced by the addition of roux is something that no self-respecting Cajun can resist.

When Mama cooked any liquid dish that involved chicken, she insisted that you cook it with bone-in chicken. It was her contention that you created the stock while you were boiling the chicken. She would begin by cutting up a whole chicken into the customary parts and placing them into a large stock pot with about 4 to 5 quarts of water into which about one pint of roux had been dissolved. She would add her coarsely chopped vegetables or mirepoix early in the boiling process to cook away and enhance the stock; however, she would also add some later in the cooking process because she liked to get the visual and textural appeal the cooked vegetables added to the final dish.

She would make the dumplings by sifting together 3 cups of flour with one teaspoon of salt, two teaspoons of baking powder and one half teaspoon of baking soda. To these sifted ingredients, she would cut in one half cup of shortening. She would then add one cup of cold milk and one tablespoon of melted butter to form a sticky dough ball that was poured out onto a floured rolling board that Mama used for her baking. She always said the you could use plenty of flour to roll out the dumplings, since you wanted them to have more body.

After the contents of the stock pot had cooked over a low boil for enough time to almost completely cook the chicken, she would add in the dumplings and simmer for about another twenty minutes or so to cook the dumplings. She would serve me a large bowl of this along with some vegetable side dishes such as fresh string beans, broccoli or corn on the cob. What a meal, but beware – this dish usually required a nap to recover afterwards.

If you are a bit adventuresome, it would behoove you to try this dish on your family and friends. If you do, you will get the opportunity to see how a bayou Cajun converts a common American dish into a Cajun creation.

Cora's Chicken and Dumplin's

INGREDIENTS:

1	Pint of Roux
4 quarts	Water

The Mirepoix:

3	Large yellow onions
4 cups	Coarsely chopped celery
2 large	Coarsely chopped green bell pepper
2-3 tbsps.	Vegetable oil
1	Whole chicken cut up into parts
1 cup	Chopped green onions
5 tsps.	Sea salt (or to taste)

Optional:

2-4	Chopped jalapenos *(not exactly Cajun but tasty)*

Coarsely chopped 2 of your 3 large yellow onions (reserve one onion for later) and combine with vegetable oil, celery and bell pepper (mirepoix) in a large stockpot over medium-high heat for a light sauté. Add water and bring to a rolling boil. Remove metal lid from the jar of roux and microwave for about 3 to 4 minutes until roux is warmed, making it melt and combine with water quicker. Spoon roux into the boiling water, stirring continuously until all of the roux is completely melted. If excess foaming occurs that cannot be controlled by continuously stirring, lower heat and continue to cook until all roux is dissolved. Add in chicken and return to a boil then lower heat to a low boil and simmer for about one half hour, stirring occasionally.

During this period, you prepare the dumplings as follows:

INGREDIENTS:

3 cups   Flour (all purpose)
½ cup   Shortening
1 cup   Milk
1 tsp.   Salt
2 tsps. Baking powder
½ tsp.   Baking soda
1 tbsp. Melted butter

Sift in all dry ingredients together in a bowl and cut in shortening with a pastry cutter. Add in cold milk and melted butter. Roll out on a floured board and cut into squares.

When chicken is almost completely cooked, the yellow onion that was reserved should be cut up in slices, separated into rings and dropped into the mixture for appearance and texture. You can additionally add a chopped red, yellow or orange bell pepper and a cup or two of coarsely chopped celery at this point for appearance and texture. Add in dumplings and return to boil, then lower heat to maintain low boil and to cook dumplings for 20 to 30 minutes. Then, turn off heat and add green onions. It is now time to serve this dish in large bowls to a group of what I hope are real hungry lumberjacks.

CHAPTER TEN

"Hold on While I Put On a Pot of Rice..."

"Hold on while I put on a pot of rice .. "

Rice is actually the edible seeds of an annual cereal grass, and is grown throughout the world. Rice is rich in carbohydrates and is the staple food for many cultures. The process of growing rice involves the flooding of fields where rice is grown during the period when the rice plants are in their adolescent stages. In addition to providing the abundance of water required by the plant to grow, being submerged during this period of their existence acts as a barrier to certain pests and diseases.

Though it can be somewhat labor-intensive to grow, rice was an agricultural product that did well in the coastal prairies and marshlands of Louisiana. The hot, humid summers and mild winters with an abundance of water seemed to provide rice a natural homeland for cultivation. Every culture seems to have a starchy food that is associated with them, and for Cajuns it would have to be rice. When I was growing up, rice was rather omnipresent. There was rice with gumbos and stews, rice and gravy, beans and rice, rice dressing, jambalaya, "dirty rice," boudain and rice pudding for desert. I was especially fond of eating hot, fresh cooked rice with cold milk poured over it. Who but a bayou Cajun would name and relish a dish called "dirty rice?"

Although rice has many types, the main categories seem to be long, medium and short grain varieties. Bayou Cajuns tend to lean towards medium and short grain rice, both of which have a tendency to be sticky when cooked. Mama had a pot that she only used for cooking rice that she called her "rice pot" (Cajuns really have a way with words). Every day we seemed to have rice, either fresh cooked or leftover, in some way or another. Mama even preferred leftover rice for certain dishes like rice and oyster dressing, and for the stir-fry dishes she often made with vegetables and shrimp, although she did not refer to them as "stir-fry." Mama always said that when "yoo put rice in da ice box" (refrigerator) overnight, it makes it better for other dishes. To this day, one of my favorite dishes is something my dad made with leftover rice, yellow onions, green onions and bell peppers that had been sautéed in the bacon grease rendered from thick, hand cut bacon, served with fried eggs on top that had also been cooked (over medium) and basted in bacon grease, and French bread (thickly buttered of course) that had been toasted under the broiler in the oven.

Even though we seemed to grow everything else, we did not grow rice in our garden. Nor did we grow wheat to produce the flour we needed; we did grow a small amount of sugar cane, but that was mostly for us kids to peel and chew for fun. Due to the difficulty to dry and mill rice and wheat, and the somewhat complex process of getting sugar from sugar cane, we traded with Mr. Schuchardt (who owned the general store in Sabine Pass) for rice, flour and sugar – usually in large bulk bags. Mama raised small chicks that Mr. Shoeheart sold at his store, and we traded those for such commodities we could not produce on a practical basis.

Riz in da Mornin'

Left-over *riz* (prounced *ree* meaning rice) was a constant commodity in most Cajun households, as it was in ours. Mama did not cook rice for a specific dish or certain amount. Her "rice pot" which was used regularly and cooked nothing else, would cook about six cups of cooked rice and Mama would cook rice anytime we had eaten all that was cooked the last time.

Most Cajuns eat rice with a lot of things so there was always some around. My Daddy loved breakfast and he cooked a left-over rice dish in the morning that he would top with fried eggs. I too became very fond of this dish and I cook it often to this day.

Cajun Fried Rice

INGREDIENTS:

6 to 8 Strips of bacon (chopped in small pieces)
1 Medium yellow onion (chopped)
1 Green bell pepper (chopped)
2 ribs Celery (chopped)
1 cup Green onions (chopped)
Cooked rice

In a large skillet, cook the bacon over medium high heat until it is brown and almost crisp; then, remove all of the excess bacon grease except about two to three tablespoons. Break the bacon into small pieces and add in the chopped onion, bell pepper and celery. Continue cooking until all vegetables are cooked but still a little crunchy, and then deglaze with a small amount of water, maybe ¼ cup or less. Lower the heat to medium and add in the cooked rice and green onions, and stir until combined with the other ingredients and rice is thoroughly heated. Remove from heat and serve a thick layer of this rice in a plate topped with two (or three... or four...) fried eggs cooked your favorite way. Add in a link of boiled, heavily-smoked sausage, and some very tough French bread that has been split open, buttered and then toasted under the broiler. Boudreaux and Theriot would say that you "be eatin' up da hog leg" (high on the hog).

Daddy loved a good breakfast, and he actually just loved breakfast food in general. We often had the above-described dish and its accompaniments for our evening meal. I can still remember my Daddy cooking this meal and singing a little French song that he often sang or whistled while he was performing a task.

The variations on this dish are endless as far as the ingredients go. My wife Dodie likes to use red, yellow and orange bell peppers in this dish (which gives it a lot of eye appeal), as well as carrots and sometimes left-over sweet peas. I have cooked it with broccoli as well, and we sometimes throw in turnips when we have some in our garden.

Shrimp Jambalaya

Jambalaya is a dish that can be made with many variations and in different ways; however, the following recipe is one my favorite ways to cook it. *Jambalaya* (popularly pronounced *jam ba lie a* but pronounced *jam ba lie* by Cajuns) is one of the Cajun dishes that has attained some degree of recognition by the general public, primarily because of cooking channels on television. My Mama called it *yumbaya* (pronounced *yum bah yah'* – bayou Cajun slang). A dish that is primarily designed around rice, jambalaya can be cooked in many different ways and with many different ingredients. Another Cajun dish called "dirty rice" is actually a form of jambalaya; however, dirty rice is usually made with cooked rice and jambalaya is made with uncooked rice.

Like many Cajun dishes, the ingredients are rather simple, so don't be enticed into believing that you need to include such things as Dijon mustard, Romano cheese, rosemary or mushrooms. You could possibly use such ingredients in your own version of jambalaya, since by its very nature, jambalaya is an evolving profusion of elements into a casserole type of dish. But Cajun jambalaya is rather simple in make-up, and only needs to include some of the Cajun basics i.e. mirepoix, green onions, cayenne pepper etc. to be called truly authentic.

You must remember that Cajuns grew or gathered most of the things that they cooked with, including their spices. Although she dried herbs for use when they were not in season, Mama preferred to use fresh herbs, so having them right out the back door was important to her, especially for dishes like jambalaya. Like most all Cajun dishes, good jambalaya is made with simple ingredients and careful preparation. Now, come with me *chere* and I will take you fa a lil' trip down yumbayah bayou:

INGREDIENTS:

2 lbs.	Small to medium shrimp – peeled and deveined
1	Large yellow onion (chopped)
1	Green bell pepper (chopped)
2 ribs	Celery (chopped)
1 cup	Green onions (chopped)
½ cup	Minced parsley (fresh)
2 cups	Medium grain rice (washed) – *brown rice also works well with this dish*
3 tbsps.	Vegetable oil
4 cups	Water *(Mama sometimes used chicken stock – si bon)*
1 clove	Garlic (minced)
	Salt to taste *(start off with about 1 tsp.)*
	Cayenne pepper to taste *(be careful chere)*

In a large cast iron skillet, combine the oil, yellow onion, bell pepper and celery and sauté over medium high heat until softened somewhat, then add in shrimp, garlic, rice, salt and cayenne. Stir for about 2 to three minutes, then add water, parsley and green onions, then cover and lower heat to a very low setting. Do not lift the cover to check this dish, since it needs to cook covered to hold the steam in to cook the rice properly. After about 20 to 25 minutes, the rice will be done, and you can remove from heat and serve. Lengthen the cooking time somewhat if you chose to use brown rice. You may have to vary the cooking time with your stove on the lowest setting to get the rice to come out just right. If you miss it and the rice burns on the bottom a little, shorten the time a few minutes. If there is still too much moisture in the bottom of the pot, then add a few minutes to the cooking time.

I encourage you to try this dish with brown rice, since the nutty flavor imparted by brown rice is especially desirable for the dish. In all of my cooking, I use brown rice exclusively. I learned to like brown rice from my Mama, who used it on some occasions. She only switched to white rice since it became cheaper as it increased in popularity with the buying public. More than likely, jambalaya was originally made with brown rice (although white rice was widely available during my lifetime, even to Cajuns).

Another variation of this dish involves substituting thin pork chops in place of the shrimp. Yet another version that Mama cooked used crawfish with brown rice, which was (and still is) one of my favorites. All of the rest of the ingredients and instructions are pretty much the same.

CHAPTER ELEVEN

CANNING WITH MAMA

Canning with Mama

Growing up on the marshlands at the tip of coastal East Texas and southwestern Louisiana was an interesting experience. Running parallel to the coastline were two natural ridges that were a foot or two above the level of the surrounding marshland. It was on these ridges in the land where all of the people that called this area home built their houses upon and lived. We lived on what was termed the "front ridge," since it was the one closest to the sea shore of the Gulf of Mexico. Although we lived on the edge of the marsh, our land was high enough above sea level to have a rather large garden on which we raised virtually everything that we ate.

Typical of coastal lands, the soil was a mix of sandy loam and clay, and was very fertile. Mama was a very adapt gardener, and we always raised plenty of corn, peas, tomatoes, peppers of all types, sweet potatoes, onions, beans of many types, cauliflower, and carrots as well as some special vegetables for our area like asparagus and peanuts. We planted a rather large garden, larger than we actually needed for ourselves, but Cora always grew enough to give away to friends or neighbors in need. She even said that you should always plant enough for the animals to get some, too. Mama never complained when the racoons ate some of the vegetables. She would always say that we have so much and that they have so little, so it did not hurt us for them to eat a little bit. To this day, when I plant a garden, I plant more than I can eat because I know that the rabbits will be there. Mama always raised lots of chickens and some pigs (*cochon* [singular] – pronounced *coo shon'*) along with goats (*cabri* [singular] – pronounced *ka brie'*) that were mostly for milk and cheese. Even though we had a small refrigerator and freezer, the bulk of our food preservation was in the form of canning.

Canning days were always a wonder of excitement for me, since I was Mama's chief assistant. We would usually tackle a single vegetable at one time for canning activities; however, sometimes Mama and I canned prepared foods, and we also canned hens (*poule* [singular] – pronounced *poo' el*). After Mama sterilized the jars, it was usually my job to fill them the way she instructed me to with whatever vegetable she wanted to do for the day. I particularly liked to do string beans and tomatoes, but I always kind of dreaded the days we did peas, since peas had to be shelled. I was always told that hard work and long tasks built character, so I was sure that I developed plenty of character on pea shelling day. My thumbs were sore for days.

The prepared foods that we canned were always things that Mama did very well. We often did a version of chicken soup that was always good. It constantly changed, since Mama varied the recipe depending upon the vegetables we had at the time (she called it "slumgullion"). We also canned turtle stew and turtle soup when Daddy was able to catch a green sea turtle in the Gulf of Mexico. Although it was not very Cajun-like, Mama did not like fresh water turtles and it was not against the law to take some sea turtles at that time. We also made what I 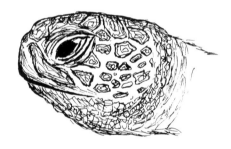 guess could be called "Cajun salsa," which Mama called "chow-chow," that was quite good. It was made with a lot of tomatoes, peppers and onions and we made a lot of it.

Of all the things we canned, I think that making pickles was my favorite canning experience, and I continue to do more pickling than any other type of canning to this day. Mama always said that you could pickle almost anything, and that is exactly what we did. The jars mostly had cucumbers in them, but she always put in other vegetables to make the jars look better and vary the taste. Sometimes, we would simply pick whatever there was in the garden, and then come in and put all of the things we could find in the garden into our jars as Mama would mix up her pickling juice to fill them. I still remember eating these impromptu pickled vegetables with a great deal of excitement and satisfaction.

The day after canning was always followed by a day of distribution where I went to all of the houses around our's and gave our neighbors some of the food we canned. As was the custom, most of the people returned our jars to us with food they had canned, but Mama was the most productive and she also was the one who enjoyed it the most. Cora was hyperactive, and if she were young today she would probably be given ADHD drugs to slow her down, but she was really just a ball of fire. A person who loved her very much and meant it in an affectionate way once said that Cora "had a bumblebee stuffed up her butt." She believed in canning enough to eat and enough to give away, and she actively and regularly practiced this principle. At the time I was not aware, but she passed that feeling and enjoyment on to me, for I can and pickle to this day, and I cannot wait for when the jars are ready to start giving to my friends and associates.

Cora on Pickling

When I was very young, I acquired a taste for just about anything that was pickled, and this was very fortunate for me since Mama was very adept at pickling. Cora pickled just about everything. This was probably the first thing that Mama taught me to do in the realm of cooking. Mama would go out into the garden and start picking a mixture of things that would go into our pickles. Even though this creation centered on the *concombre* (pronounced *ko' kom* meaning cucumber), Mama would create a mélange of different vegetables in every jar. To the cucumbers, she would sometimes add green cherry tomatoes, banana peppers, cayenne peppers, okra, carrots, string beans, asparagus, baby ears of corn on the cob, onions (both sliced and small, whole), garlic, bird's eye pepper, and or anything else that would tolerate pickling. Most often, it was whatever we could find in the garden. Cora always grew an abundance of fresh dill, the seeds and foliage of which she used in her pickled vegetables. Mama capitalized on the innate curiosity of a child (coupled with my love of pickles) to teach me how to make them. The child within Cora was omnipresent and ever-vigilant for an opportunity to reach into your soul, and implant the abilities and heritage she had assembled in her life. Because she was Cajun, much of her knowledge was in the form of cooking, and like all things Cora knew, she was anxious to share with others.

A born teacher, Mama had a way of giving you her undivided attention. As I watched her later in life interacting with my children, it made me remember her doing things like sitting down on the floor to read to me, our many cooking sessions, or stopping her daily activities to show how to do something that would be considered by others to be insignificant. Cora did not think that any child's question or wonderment was insignificant; moreover, she viewed it as an opportunity to enlighten that which fate had inadvertently provided – a moment in time. To this day, I still pickle many vegetables the same way Mama taught me, and I used the same fascination to pass on the recipes and methods to my sons. It appears that Cora taught me not only how to make pickles but how to teach someone to make pickles.

My apologies to you for digressing when I talk about Mama, but it appears that age provides the pathway to understanding and appreciating those things that life imposes on you. One day, you discover that it was not an imposition at all, but actually the bits and pieces of your heritage and existence; the things that make you at peace with yourself and who you really are. It is hard to believe that I derived all of this from making pickles, but life does not always speak directly to us.

To make good pickles, you first have to get past the thought that only cucumbers can be pickled. In fact, almost any vegetable can be successfully pickled, and most vegetables can be used to enhance the cucumbers you pickle. I would never consider pickling cucumbers without some form of pepper added (cayenne, bird's eye, etc.) and usually also including onion slices (yellow, sweet) and maybe a garlic clove or two. Mama stressed also the assembly of the vegetables in the jar as an important step. She would say that you are going to be looking at the jars on the shelf for a lot longer than the time you spend eating the pickles, so the presentation was important. When she had placed enough cucumbers in the jars to hold everything in place, she would slide sliced vegetables down the side of the jar so that they would show after the pickles were completed. Mama talked at length about the importance of the colors and textures that you would be able to see through the sides of the jar. She would place things like carrot slices, red pepper slices, yellow pepper slices, purple bird's eye peppers, and anything else for color contrasts.

If you would like to try your hand at pickling (and I sincerely hope you do), the following is a recipe that has worked well for me as well as my Mama.

Cora's Pickling Juice

INGREDIENTS:

64 oz. Water

32 oz. Distilled white vinegar

¾ cup Pickling salt *(do not use regular salt)*

½ tsp. Dill seeds (per jar)

½ tsp. Peppercorns (per jar) – *I like tri-color but black will do*
      Dill foliage

The traditional method (which I use) makes enough for about 4 to 5 quarts of pickled vegetables: Sterilize jars and add dill seeds and pepper corns to bottom of each jar. Wash vegetables and pack in jars with dill foliage (for appearance). Bring water, vinegar and salt to rolling boil in a large sauce pan, and immediately remove from heat and fill jars with hot liquid to the top. Insert a plastic spatula down the sides of the jars to remove air bubbles, then refill to top. Tighten lids and let cool. Check all lids for vacuum then store in a cool place away from sunlight. I have used this method all of my life making pickled vegetables for my family and friends without experiencing any ill effects. In an abundance caution, I am not going to recommend this method to you, the reader, and instead refer you to the USDA recommended, germophobic, water bath method.

The water bath method is as follows: There is a pot and jar rack made specifically for this method, and it can be used for canning other types of products. Do all of the above except, when filling with hot liquid, leave one inch space (head space) at top of jars, and then do not tighten lids as much. Immerse in a hot water bath and boil for 5 to 10 minutes. Heat from the boiling water will force air from the jars leaving a vacuum seal on lids. Remove, cool and store as directed.

CHAPTER TWELVE

COTTON'S SEAFOOD –
THE BUSINESS

Cotton's Seafood – The Business

Cotton and Cora ran the family business, Cotton's Seafood, differently than most typical Cajun fishing families. Although the business philosophy of catching, processing and selling directly to the consuming public was not invented by Cotton and Cora, it was definitely perfected by them. Cotton would not sell any seafood that he was not prepared to eat himself, a fact that he proclaimed often. As a matter of fact, I can remember distinctly on a few occasions where Cotton would remark that some remaining shrimp had been on ice for a day or so and were thus "not fresh enough to sell," so Cotton would tell Cora to boil them and we would eat them ourselves. It's funny how, when I say "Cotton and Cora," it sounds so right – since they were such a unique and obvious set of individuals. One could hardly think of either one of them without thinking of the other. They were married for over sixty years, until Cotton died, and Cora still sat next to him in his truck when they rode down the highway.

As far as the business of the business went, Cora was the money handler and deal maker. Cotton was strictly the producer. Cotton caught and processed whatever seafood they were selling at the time, and Cora made the sale and took the money. Cotton never exhibited any type of pretense over the arrangement, since his stoic nature was to accept and operate under the best circumstances that were available without delving into the "can, would, could, should" of a given situation. I can still remember Cotton going to Cora telling her he needed some amount of money for some part for his boat or whatever, and Cora handing him the money he requested. Mama paid all of the bills, and anytime we had an unexpected problem or needed money for something, she would come up with the money from somewhere. Cora had money in small quantities stashed everywhere. Although

I felt like we were poor, especially compared to other kids and their families, we always had everything we really needed; mostly though, we had Cotton and Cora.

Cotton was very proud of his seafood products; a fact that he proclaimed endlessly. From the moment that he caught the seafood, it was heavily iced down for holding until sale. Cora worked on the boat, assisting with the culling of the catch and with the cleaning and preparation of seafood items caught in the net other than shrimp (called "by-catch"). The by-catch was usually crabs, along with some soft-shelled crabs and flounder that were either sold or given as *lagniappe* (pronounced *lan yap'* and meaning a little something extra). Cora had a way of endearing people to her in life that filtered through into the business. Cora and Cotton would sprinkle their discourse to customers with Cajun French culture, and Cora would tell stories of her past and growing up in a family of trappers and commercial fishermen. Their customers adored them, and bought whatever seafood that they had at the time. Once Cora assessed the catch of the day, she would get on the telephone to people she had on a customer list, and the catch was usually sold before we even finished unloading the boat. Cora always had something cooking on the stove, and it usually included something that was being sold. Cora would give the customer a small bowl of whatever she had cooking for them to try. A favorite with customers was Cora's jambalaya. I remember once when a lady (who had been buying seafood from my Mama for what seemed like always) told me that she felt like she was part of the family when she was around Cotton and Cora, and that they were very dear to her.

Cotton's boats that he used over the years were always ones that he built himself, and they seemed to get progressively bigger and better than the previous ones had been. The last boat he had was a twenty-seven foot aluminum hull with a small cabin forward. It was launched from a trailer, since that was a later requirement for all of Cotton's boats. He did not like leaving his boat in the water when not in use because he said it caused too many maintenance problems. Cotton used the same boat for oystering, crabbing and shrimping. It was just a matter of re-rigging the boat for a different activity.

Cotton's last boat

The prospect of going out with Cotton on his boat was not something that was usually contemplated. Other than Mama and me, and later on my wife, Dodie, and sometimes a close friend of mine, Jim Mayer, I do not remember anybody else ever going on a shrimping expedition with Cotton. Jim Mayer is a guitar friend (and a very close friend) of mine who came from Colorado. After coming down several times to eat with me at Mama's and visiting with the folks, Jim adopted Cotton and Cora as his folks (away from home), and was constantly after me to go to "Cotton and Cora's" and go out on the boat. After getting to know him, Cotton was moved to say that Jim Mayer was living proof that "Coonasses were made and not born."

I can still remember Cotton saying that if you go out with him, you have to be willing to stay if he is catching shrimp. Shrimping, unlike most of Cotton's other quarry, was a rather opportunistic venture, and you had to be ready to stay the course when you were catching them in some degree of quantity. Although Cotton was very good at his craft, even he on rare occasion would return after a shrimping trip empty-handed, since this is the very nature of this endeavor.

Galahad

The only person that I ever knew Cotton taking a special interest in going out on his boat with was my wife, along with a dog that we had when we married named Galahad. Dodie and Cotton seemed to develop a special relationship from the day they met. Cotton was always bringing Dodie soft shelled crabs and flounder, which he knew she especially liked. He also asked her if we were "coming down to go out on the boat this weekend." Dodie also liked going out on Cotton's boat, since it was a rather unique activity to which the general public was not usually exposed. The real surprise relationship was between Cotton and our dog Galahad.

Galahad was a registered silver-grey sable German Shepherd. He was rather large for the breed at 125 pounds. Aside from his striking appearance, Galahad was probably the most disciplined dog that I had ever known. In retrospect, his ability to take correction was probably a function of the fact that I spent a large amount of time with him as a puppy. When I got him, I did not know anything about raising dogs, so I just raised him like I would a child. I spoke to him in whole sentences and I corrected him consistently, and he grew to be a dog that was a pleasure to be around. Even though Galahad was bigger than Dodie, he minded her and reacted to her like she was his Mama. To Cotton, a dog as big and beautiful as Galahad (and was well-disciplined) was a wonder to behold. When we were at Cotton and Cora's house, Cotton would go outside and visit with Galahad, and they would "pal around together" while Cotton worked on his net or re-rigged his boat, or whatever other activity Cotton might have been doing at the time. Cotton liked having Galahad go out on the boat with us, and he even let him ride up on the bow of the boat. Everyone who knew Cotton was amazed by the relationship that evolved between he and Galahad.

Cora's Shrimp & Crab Stew

Mama made a dish that was so over-the-top good that I struggle to describe how wonderful it actually was. She called it shrimp and crab stew, although I suppose that it was not a true "stew" in that it did not have the attributes of what is more commonly called a stew in regular cooking circles. It is actually just a thicker, richer, more intense gumbo. It was, however, the name given to this dish by my Mama, Cora LaBove, a real Cajun belle and bayou queen, and that was good enough for me.

Recreating this dish is another problem, primarily because of scarcity and cost of the ingredients. When Mama made this dish, she did not use whole crab bodies; she only used blue crab meat, and a lot of it. Having a large amount of crab meat around all of the time was no problem for us growing up, since we caught blue crabs virtually every day. Mama would boil three or four dozen crabs when the boat came in, and cooled them off to be refrigerated. We would then pick out the crabs that had been refrigerated the night before, since

Cotton's first shrimp boat, the "Inez B," circa 1947

crab meat was easier to pick when the crabs had been in the ice box for a night. After dinner we would sit around visiting and picking out the crab meat before bedtime. We did not do this every night, but we did it quite often. So often in fact that one time Mama told me and Daddy that she had just checked the freezer, and that we had

Cotton and Jim with two unknown persons, circa 1948

to start eating crab meat since she had counted over 70 lbs we had on hand. We never sold crab meat, even though it would have been quite profitable. Crab meat fell in a category that included soft-shelled crabs, green sea turtle (when it was legal to take them), pompano and grouper: things Mama and Daddy said were reserved for ourselves to eat, and not for sale. They both felt that although we were of meager circumstances, we could have some things that were somewhat extravagant and strictly our own.

The high cost of crabmeat and the large amount used in Mama's shrimp and crab stew added to the amazement of the satisfying taste of the dish. Mama would bring about 5 to 6 quarts of water in a large stock pot to a boil, and dissolve one quart of roux in the water. She would then add the mirepoix to the mixture, along with a handful of shrimp and a handful of crabmeat. She would simmer this mixture at a gentle boil for about an hour and a half to two hours (until it had somewhat reduced). She said that it needed to reduce, since the shrimp would give off some water when they were introduced to cook in the mixture. She would then add about 5 pounds of peeled shrimp and cook for a few minutes until the shrimp were done; then she would add 6 or 7 pounds of crab meat, and as soon as the stew returned to a boil, she would add about a cup of fresh parsley and about two cups of chopped green onions. She would then turn off the fire, and the dish was done (since the crab meat was cooked before it

Cotton overseeing the construction of one of his shrimp boats, circa 1974

got into the dish). Mama's preferred method of serving this dish was with some of her home-made French bread, but I usually chose to eat it over rice that had been dusted with filé, along with a couple of hard-boiled eggs.

I do have to admit that accompanying shrimp and crab stew with Mama's French bread was a truly superb way to enjoy this dish. I still can recall the smell that filled the house when Mama was baking French bread, which she usually did two times a week when I was very young. Mama always used cake yeast, which seemed to have a fuller aroma to me. Her French bread was among the best that I have ever tasted. The soft, doughy inner bread was covered by a tough, chewy outer crust. It was the perfect accompaniment for Mama's shrimp and crab stew.

I have already said Cora's Shrimp and Crab Gumbo was one of my favorite things that Mama cooked, but her Shrimp and Crab Stew was my all-time favorite dish. It was so rich from all of the crabmeat and concentrated roux that my Daddy used to say that "it made your teeth hurt." The flavor of Mama's rich, dark roux coupled with the inherent richness of crab meat is something that cannot be described with mere words – it has to be experienced to fully understand. To this day, I have never cooked this dish for anyone who was not floored by its richness and flavor. When Mama would cook this for me, I would eat it for breakfast, dinner (lunch) and supper, until it was all gone. Not long after Dodie and I were married, Mama cooked a shrimp and crab stew for us one weekend when we went to visit her and Daddy. The dish instantly became Dodie's favorite thing, and was frequently used by my Daddy to lure Dodie and me down to visit them. Cotton would say, "Dodie, Cora is goin' to cook a shrimp and crab stew this weekend – are ya'll comin'?" At this point, I felt like a politician being pursued by an aggressive lobbyist. I can honestly say that it was strictly because of our visits to Mama and Daddy's that Dodie and I fought the "battle of the bulge" during the early years of our marriage.

For those of you adventurous souls who are drawn like a moth to a flame to good food, I have a recipe of Mama's shrimp and crab stew that I think you will love. Although crabs are scarcer today than they were when I was growing up, the following recipe is still something you can enjoy if you can go crabbin' and catch about three or four dozen blue crabs, and if you have the fortitude to sit and pick out the meat. If catching and picking out the crabmeat sounds a bit formidable to you, feel free to purchase the meat already picked out, but be forewarned – this is not an inexpensive dish.

Cora's Shrimp and Crab Stew

INGREDIENTS:

1 quart	Roux
6 quarts	Water

The Mirepoix:

3	Large yellow onions
4	Cups of coarsely chopped celery
2	Large coarsely chopped green bell pepper
4 lbs.	Small to medium peeled shrimp
5 lbs.	Blue crabmeat *(more if you dare, up to 7 lbs.)*
1 cup	Chopped green onions
½ cup	Chopped fresh parsley
2-3 tbsps.	Vegetable oil
5 tsps.	Sea salt (or to taste)
1	Loaf French bread
1	Dozen eggs
	Filé to taste

Optional:

  2-4   Chopped jalapenos *(not exactly Cajun but tasty)*

  1-2 tsps.   Cayenne pepper *(very Cajun)*

  1-2 Pods   Minced garlic *(I like it without garlic)*

Coarsely chop 2 of your 3 large yellow onions (reserve one onion for later) and combine with vegetable oil, celery and bell pepper (mirepoix) and your choice of pepper (if desired) in a large stockpot over medium-high heat for a light sauté. Add water and bring to a rolling boil. Remove metal lid from the jar of roux and microwave for about 2 to 3 minutes, until roux is warmed (warming the roux makes it melt and combine with the water quicker). Spoon roux into the boiling water, stirring continuously, until all of the roux is completely melted. If excess foaming occurs that cannot be controlled by continuously stirring, then lower heat and continue until all roux is dissolved. Due to the concentration of the roux compared to water mixed into this recipe, extra care should be exercised to make sure that all of the roux is dissolved before you begin the simmer stage. Any amount of roux that is left undissolved could attach to the bottom of the pot and start to burn, and could potentially ruin the dish. At this point, a handful of shrimp and a handful of crabmeat should be added to flavor the liquid during the simmering process. Lower heat to achieve a gentle boil, and simmer for about one hour, stirring occasionally.

Boil one dozen eggs in a sauce pan until hard boiled. Crack and peel eggs. Reserve for later use when serving the stew.

After simmering, the shrimp should be added to the mixture and the heat elevated to return the mixture to a boil. The yellow onion that was reserved should be cut up in slices, separated into rings and dropped into the mixture for appearance and texture. You can additionally add a chopped red, yellow or orange bell pepper at this point. Then, lower heat to maintain low boil and to cook shrimp for about 10 to 15 minutes. Add crabmeat (if cooked already), and as soon as mixture returns to a boil, turn off heat and add parsley and green onions. If raw crabmeat is used, cook an additional 5 to 10 minutes. Serve with French bread or if desired, over cooked rice dusted with filé and one or two peeled, hard boiled eggs.

French Bread – Cora Style

I have distinct recollections about Mama's French bread. The aroma of yeast would permeate the air of our tiny home on French bread day, which usually occurred about two days per week. Mama would bake enough bread for us to have in between those times, along with anything else that she wanted to bake. Especially during the summer months, baking meant heating up the house, which was not insulated and definitely not air conditioned. Even though it sounds rather intolerable in this day and age where refrigerated air is so ubiquitous that it is accepted as a basic necessity, no one else we knew had air conditioning, so we did not know to miss it. In looking back, I do not remember the lack of air conditioning ever being a factor in our everyday lives. You cannot long for that which you are not aware. When the yeast would begin to make the bread dough rise, it would give off a familiar olfactory sensation that alerted me and my sisters to the fact that hot French bread was on the way.

When you describe the qualities that make good French bread to anyone who is not Cajun, you start to feel like you are relating the results of a failed bread-making attempt to someone. To a bayou Cajun, good French bread has a very tough crust that (if you make it right) has to be torn apart firmly with both hands. The inner bread is very soft, and has large holes that result from minimal kneading. The yeasty smell and taste augments the simple ingredients used in its construction. In my early failed attempts to make French bread, it seldom came out like Mama's, and her response to me when seeking her advice on how to fix it was usually the same. She would usually say "Jimmy, you 'r tryin' to mak it too good *chere*; it is only flour, yeast, oil and water." She would say that you should not put in eggs, milk and other things if you want to make good French bread.

Mama would start off with cake yeast, since she felt that it was the freshest and best yeast you could get. When I was young, dehydrated yeast was not available, at least not to us. The only yeast you seemed to be able to get was cake yeast, which had to be refrigerated to keep it inactive. It came wrapped in foil, and was about the size of two pats of butters. Mama would usually start off by placing about ¼ cup of warm water into a large glass along, with about two teaspoons of pure cane syrup and two yeast cakes. The yeast cakes would start to dissolve as they warmed up, and the little yeast critters would somewhat quickly become very active as they started to wake up and eat the syrup while exhaling alcohol gas. After a few minutes, the glass would have become full of a heavy foam mixture that seemed to be expanding before your eyes, and you knew it was ready for use.

While she was waiting for the yeast to become active, she was measuring out and mixing her dry ingredients, and measuring her wet ingredients in preparation for combining it all to make the dough. Mama would start off by placing about 12 cups of all purpose flour (preferably unbleached) into a large mixing bowl along with about four teaspoons of salt. After thoroughly combining those dry ingredients, she would make a "well" (an indention) into the dry mixture to hold the wet ingredients, and add in 5 cups of slightly warmed water, about 1 cup of oil and the activated yeast. The reason she would use lightly warmed water was so that the yeast would continue to be active. She would start out mixing the dough with a spoon, but rather quickly would change to her hands as the dough ball started to form and get thick. Mama would sometimes add a small amount of flour to the dough while she was mixing until it stopped sticking to her hands. She would then turn the dough out onto a floured surface and then knead it for a short period. Next, she would form the dough into a ball, tucking the edges around the back side and placing it back into the original mixing bowl, into which she would pour about a ¼ cup of oil. After coating the top of the dough ball with oil, she would turn the bottom side over into the bowl and set it on the back of the stove to rise, covered with a kitchen towel. The stove was always a warm place since we had a butane stove with pilot lights which burned constantly.

After about an hour, the dough would have doubled in size and would then be turned out again onto the flour surface for kneading, but only for about one minute. Mama would then cut the dough into about four even pieces. Each piece would then be rolled until it formed a cylinder about three inches in diameter and about 18" long. Then, she would take two of the cylinders of bread dough and twist them around each other about three times, pinch the ends together, tuck it under the loaf on each end, and place it on a baking sheet that was oiled and dusted with flour. She would do the same with the other two cylinders of dough, making two large loves of French bread. These two loves would then be allowed to rise again for about an hour.

After the second rise and just prior to going into the oven for baking, Mama would take a single edged razor blade and cut the top surface of each twist of bread dough about a ¼ inch deep, dust both loaves with flour, and place in a heated, 375 deg. F oven for about 40 minutes. Offset to one side on a lower rack, Mama had placed a cast iron skillet prior to pre-heating the oven. Immediately after placing the bread into the oven, she would pour about ¼ cup of water into the cast iron skillet and close the oven door to capture the steam that this produced. This steam created in the oven is what made the outer edge of the bread tough (a desirable trait). As the end of the cooking time was approaching, Mama would tap on the loaves listening for a hollow sound that signaled when the loaves were done.

When the French bread came out of the oven, the loaves were golden brown and beautiful. The loaves Mama made were fat in the middle and the ends came to a smaller, rounded point. The places Mama made the cuts with the razor blade allowed the bread to burst open and expand out for a beautiful presentation. As I am writing, I feel like I can smell it now – oh, that hot, yeasty bread smell – *si bon*. Somehow, as if by some primal instinct, my sisters and I seemed to know exactly when the bread was done, because we would all come to the kitchen and began lobbying Mama for some hot bread when it was ready. Mama was a pushover, and we knew she would let us have hot French bread dripping with fresh butter. Thinking about it takes me back to Mama's little kitchen and the sight of her kneading the dough on our kitchen table. She would often sing a French song while she was working, cooking, cleaning... Recalling those times warms my mind and body. I wish Mama knew I was writing about her cooking – maybe she does. After much trial and error, I finally was able to reproduce Mama's French bread in an acceptable manner. The recipe goes something like this:

French Bread – Cora Style

INGREDIENTS:

6 cups	All-purpose flour *(unbleached preferably)*
2 ½ cups	Warm water
½ cup	Vegetable oil
2 tsps.	Salt
1 pkg.	Dry, active yeast
1 tsp.	Pure cane syrup

Begin by placing the package of dry yeast into a large cup with about two tablespoons of warm water and one teaspoon of pure cane syrup. Set aside to activate.

Combine all of the other ingredients in a large mixing bowl, working with your hands until you have a heavy dough ball. If you have a mixer with a dough hook, the job becomes much easier. Turn the dough ball out onto a floured surface and knead for about one to two minutes. Pour a small amount of cooking oil into a large mixing bowl and coat the top of the kneaded dough ball with oil, and turn the bottom into the bowl for the first rise. Cover with a towel and place in a warm spot for about one hour or so (until the dough has doubled in size).

Again, turn out onto a floured surface and knead for less than one minute. It is the relatively short kneading times that create larger, irregular holes in the bread, which is a sure sign of authentically Cajun French bread. Then, cut the dough into about two equal pieces and form two cylinders of dough about 18 inches long. Twist the two cylinders two or three turns and pinch the ends together, and then tuck under the new formed loaf. Place the bread onto a cookie sheet that has been oiled and dusted with flour and let rise again for about one hour. Then make cuts about ¼ inch deep into the top of the bread twists with a sharp knife, dust both loaves with flour, and bake for about 35 to 45 minutes in a 375 deg. F. preheated oven that has a cast iron skillet placed off to one side on a lower rack. After placing the loaves into the oven, pour about ¼ cup of water into the heated cast iron skillet and close the oven door to capture the steam. Loaf should sound hollow when tapped, indicating it is done.

There were two finishes for the surface of the bread that can be used. Mama's (and my) favorite was a floury, dusty surface that resulted from sprinkling flour on the baking pan and the surface of the newly formed loaf prior to placing it in the oven for baking. Another approach was the shiny surface, which was achieved by brushing the surface of the newly-formed loaf just prior to baking with one egg beaten with 2 teaspoons of water.

The tough outer crust of Mama's French Bread is perfect for soppin' up some of her famous (at least with us) Shrimp and Crab Stew.

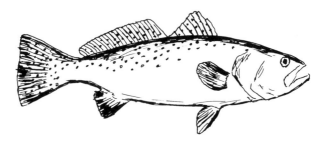

Cotton's Fried Fish

Another food technique that Cotton did very well was frying fish. My sisters and I always looked forward to Cotton's fried fish, especially since the fish he was frying were usually always just caught (and there always were a lot of them). Because the shrimp boat was a trawler, we always caught an abundance of flounder, speckled trout and red fish (the Cajun grand slam). All of these fish lend themselves particularly well to frying. I can still remember the smell of fresh frying fish coming from the work shed where Cotton liked to fry. He had made a cooking area for Cora to use while we were preparing our catch for market, and this was his preferred place to fry fish and shrimp. One of the most critical things to watch when one is frying fish is the temperature of the oil. The temperature of the oil needs to be remain between 350 deg. F and 380 deg. F for the best results. Cotton used to throw a kitchen match into the oil; when it got to the right temperature, the match would ignite. I watched him fry fish many times and marveled at how he got such great results with such basic and sparse cooking equipment.

When asked about his technique, he would respond that you need to constantly observe the bubbles around the fish you are frying and keep the fire such that the bubbles are consistent for each piece of fish during the cooking process. We always had butane gas stoves, so you were able to control the heat going to the frying pot very well. He said that you always needed enough oil for the seafood to float and not touch the bottom of the frying pot. He would show me how, when the bubbles diminished to a certain point, the fish was done and needed to be taken out of the oil to drain excess oil off (usually on newspaper). Cotton's fried fish was always just right – I can vividly remember the taste right now as I recall those times when I would watch him in anticipation of the fine eating that was shortly to come. Though it may be unhealthy, I cannot resist fried fish to this day.

When frying Cajun style, cast iron is the pot of choice since it holds heat well, and a high temperature oil like vegetable oil is required. Cotton liked to fry in an old cast iron skillet with very high sides that was made for cooking on an open fire, presumably from the chuck wagon days of yesteryear. Yesteryear was the order of the day with most of our cookware. It was a mis-match conglomeration of things that looked like they belonged in a junkyard. Upon close inspection, however, they were actually each selected for optimum use in their function, with no attention given as to their appearance or visual compatibility with anything else. Most pieces were acquired as hand-me-downs or through trading (in which Cotton and Cora were constantly engaged). Bayou Cajuns liked to trade and engage in other transactions that did not involve money. It was not that they did not like money; moreover, it probably evolved from the fact that bayou Cajuns throughout their history in southeastern Louisiana had very little money, and in their early history had little need for it. Bayou Cajuns traded for almost everything they needed that was outside of their ability to trap, harvest and gather.

Cotton was the consummate bayou Cajun, and where he got his frying pot I'm sure we will never know, but as with everything else he and Cora had, it worked perfectly for his designated use for it. Since we do not have Cotton's pot to fry in, let me suggest a cast iron dutch oven bottom, since it has high sides to contain the oil as it bubbles during frying. Also, I recommend that you acquire a frying thermometer, since throwing a kitchen match into the oil to ignite for frying temperature is likely not your style.

INGREDIENTS:

3 lbs.   Fish fillets
1 can   Evaporated milk
1 lb.   Coarse ground corn meal *(stone ground is si bon)*
           Salt to taste
           Cayenne pepper to taste

About one hour before you plan to begin cooking, rinse and pat dry your fish fillets and place them in a bowl with the evaporated milk. I like to add the cayenne pepper to the evaporated milk and stir it well before I add in the fillets. When all of the fillets have been added, place the bowl in the refrigerator for about ½ hour prior to cooking.

Select a cooking vessel that is about four inches deep (or deeper) so that you can pour in about two inches of oil and still have sufficient height left to contain the bubbling oil during frying. Begin heating the oil over high heat until a temperature of about 360 deg. F is attained.

While the oil is heating, you pour the cornmeal into a large baking pan (I use a 9" X 13"), remove the fillets from the refrigerator and begin battering them in preparation to frying. Using the "wet hand/dry hand" method, you remove a fillet with your wet hand and coat it thoroughly with cornmeal with the dry hand, until you have enough battered to load your cooking vessel. Once you have put the first load into the oil, you can be battering the next batch to go into the hot oil. It's important to remember that in order to maintain the proper cooking temperature; you have to have some battered fillets ready to immediately put in when you take the cooked fillets out. As you take the fillets out of the oil, place them on paper towels to absorb the excess oil and salt to taste while they are still very hot.

Whole Fried Fish

Cajuns love fried fish, and they love to fry fish whole as opposed to filleted. This, by description, applies to smaller fish, and is also limited to those fish that are not so inherently oily, such as mackerel or ling, where cooking them bone-in is a problem. Because of the limitation of frying pan sizes, we are primarily referring to fish in the one pound to three pound range, plus or minus. The types of fish that I grew up frying whole are: Speckled trout, flounder, red snapper, whitting and pompano. Although there are other varieties of fish that are suitable for frying whole, these are the ones that I always liked prepared in this manner. The listed varieties also have the best tasting skin when fried. Since we have already discussed the method of frying fish (which is basically the same for all fish) we should turn our attention to the preparation of the different species prior to cooking.

We are going to assume that you have caught your own fish, or were given fish by a friend or neighbor, and you thus have to start from scratch. Obviously, if you buy your fish from a seafood vendor, much of the cleaning we are going to describe will not be necessary. So you are at present looking at a whole, uncleaned fish. The initial step in preparing fish is to remove the scales. The best tool to use for this purpose is simply a tablespoon. A tablespoon does not tear into the skin as much as the fish scalers that you buy seem to do. You begin by grasping the head of the fish very firmly with one hand and scraping the scales with the edge of the tablespoon from the tail towards the head with the other hand. This is a repetitive process involving many passes with the spoon to finally remove all of the scales, especially around the fins, but care should be taken to ensure that you get all of the scales removed.

Next, with a very sharp knife, cut off
the head, exposing the abdominal cavity
and the entrails of the fish. Remove the
entrails, and split the flap of flesh at the
bottom of the abdominal cavity from where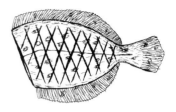
you removed the head until the cavity ends. You now have one step left
before your fish is completely cleaned. Even if you buy cleaned fish from
the market, this final step will likely not have been already done. Turn
the fish upside down and part the flaps of the abdominal cavity, exposing
the backbone of the fish. You will note a thin membrane covering what
appears to be coagulated blood along the backbone of the fish. You
now need to cut this membrane with a knife and scrape the coagulated
blood with the point of the knife, and flush it out with water until it is
practically all gone. Without this final step in cleaning, your fried fish
could have a strong fishy taste that can be unattractive.

Before we continue, we have to talk about leaving the head on
for the sake of presentation. Cooking a whole fish with the head on
certainly makes for a striking presentation to your guests. It does,
however, present another problem, and that is simply a matter of
available space. If your fish is small enough for you to leave the head on
and still fit into the frying vessel that you have selected for that purpose,
then by all means, leave the head on if you like. Available space was
not usually a problem for us, since Daddy often fried dish out in the
seafood processing room where we had a rather large burner that he had
fashioned out of an old hot water heater burner and a piece of pipe, on
which he had welded legs and a resting place for a very large cast iron
pot. Even with this excess of space, Daddy usually removed the head
since aesthetics were considered an unnecessary frivolity by Cotton. If it
were not functional, then it was not something with which Cotton was
usually interested in providing, but basically, this was the Cajun way.

Head-on or without the head, the next step is to score the fish just prior to frying. Scoring a fish involves making cuts in the flesh down to the bone at various intervals, to make it convenient to eat and to allow for more uniform cooking of thicker fish. I like scored fish since it allows for more of the corn meal to coat the fish flesh. I prefer to score my fish with a diagonal "X" fashion, but that is solely up to you. Our fish is now ready to fry.

INGREDIENTS:

2	Whole fish – scaled and cleaned
1 can	Evaporated milk
4 cups	Coarse ground corn meal *(stone ground is si bon)*
	Salt to taste
	Cayenne pepper to taste

About one hour before you plan to begin cooking, place the cleaned fish in a bowl with the evaporated milk. I like to add the cayenne pepper to the evaporated milk and stir it well before I add in the fish. I then place the bowl in the refrigerator for about ½ hour prior to cooking.

Select a cooking vessel that is deep like a cast iron, dutch oven bottom, so that you can pour in about two or three inches of oil and still have sufficient height left to contain the bubbling oil during frying.

Begin heating the oil over high heat until a temperature of about 360 deg. F is attained (a frying thermometer is recommended). While the oil is heating, pour the cornmeal into a large baking pan (I use a 9" X 13"), remove the fish from the refrigerator and begin battering them in preparation to frying, using the "wet hand/dry hand" method.

I would recommend only frying one fish at a time since it is best not to overload the cooking vessel. As we have discussed in the past, it is important to remember that in order to maintain the proper cooking temperature, you must have the next fish battered and ready to immediately put in when you take the other fish out. As you take the fish out of the oil, place it on paper towels to absorb the excess oil and salt to taste while they are still very hot.

Cotton's Chili

Cotton was not as prolific a cook as Cora, but there were a few things that he cooked well, and chili was one of them. Some of the dishes that he excelled at were learned from his days working on the big offshore shrimping vessels. Crew members would often alternate days cooking; however, after Cotton took a turn cooking, he was more often than not elected as the designated cook. The cook on one of the big shrimpers would have to divide his time between cooking and other duties, so "one pot wonders" where frequently employed. I also worked on the offshore shrimp boats (referred to as the "big boats") as a way to earn money for college during the summer, so I am very familiar with the routine employed by the designated cook. My cooking experience with my Mama made me the popular cook when I was in that situation as well.

The big boats often had stoves that were strange to the average person. Although some of the older shrimpers were equipped with diesel powered stoves, most the boats I was on were usually powered by butane gas. Each stove was equipped with a rack to hold the pots during days with rough seas. Sometimes on days with very rough seas, what you were cooking would often end up "on the deck" (floor).

My time as cook taught me that Cotton must have liked to cook, because one would have to like it somewhat to endure the rigors of cooking on the big boats while simultaneously performing your other duties. For all of the mentioned reasons, the cook's job was not very coveted. My experience was the same as Cotton's; however, we both learned that if the other crew members liked your cooking well enough, they would be happy to pitch in with the cleaning to keep you cooking.

Cotton's chili was a favorite with me and my sisters. We particularly liked it when he made it with some of the more unconventional meat ingredients, such as deer or feral hog. One of my uncles owned a large farm in the big thicket of east Texas. We traded seafood for things that my uncle hunted or raised there. We raised chickens and hogs ourselves, but feral hogs were leaner and lent themselves well to outdoor cooking and smoking. My uncle made smoked sausage with deer meat and feral hog which was especially good. He also made an unsmoked version of deer and feral hog sausage that was Daddy's favorite for his chili. I learned how to cook chili from Cotton, and his recipe went something like this:

INGREDIENTS:

1 lb.	Meat*
2	Medium yellow onions
1	Medium green bell pepper
2-4	Jalapeño peppers
5 tbsp.	Chili Power (dark)
3 tbsp.	Cumin
½ tbsp.	Oregano

1 clove Garlic

1 ½ tbsp. Paprika

1 tbsp. Salt

½ tbsp. Cayenne pepper

1 tbsp. Whole wheat flour (dissolved in 1 cup of cold water)

8 oz. Tomato sauce (usually 1 can)

16 ozs. Canned tomatoes – diced (usually 1 can)

Enough water for proper texture

Assembly & Cooking: In a large sauté pan brown meat (if raw). If you are using cooked meat, then sauté chopped onions and all peppers. Transfer to a chili pot and combine all ingredients, except the flour, over medium heat. It is at this point that you should add water to adjust the texture. Mixture should have sufficient water to cover the solid ingredients – this however is a matter of personal taste. After the amount of water is adjusted, you should bring to a slight boil and lower heat to simmer, checking water content and stirring occasionally, and adding water where necessary as contents reduce.

After the mixture has simmered for enough time to tenderize the particular type of meat you have used, it is time to add the flour/water mixture to thicken the chili. The mixture should be returned to a boil and simmered for about five minutes to cook the flour. Chili will then be ready to eat. This thickening process is not a necessary step, and can be omitted if desired.

The meat used can be of several types or combination of types: ground meat, stew meat, pork sausage (pattie), deer sausage (pattie), ground deer or ground wild pig, etc.

I have made this chili many times, and always with very good results. Over the years, I have modified it somewhat to suit the tastes of my family, who tend to like dishes with more spice heat. During the sauté stage, I add two or three Serrano peppers for heat, and usually a pablano pepper for texture. I also like the added flavor that dried onions and garlic seem to bring to the dish. My version of Cotton's Chili goes like this:

INGREDIENTS

1 lb.	Meat – ground, top sirloin, smoked meat, etc.
2	Medium yellow onions chopped
1	Medium green bell pepper chopped
1	Medium yellow bell pepper chopped
2-3	Serrano peppers split lengthwise
1	Pablano pepper chopped
1-2	Jalapeño peppers sliced
5 tbsp.	Chili Power (dark)
3 tbsp.	Cumin
½ tbsp.	Oregano
5 tbsp.	Dried Onion
½ tbsp.	Dried garlic (optional)
1 ½ tbsp.	Paprika
1 tbsp.	Sea salt
1 tbsp.	Whole wheat flour (dissolved in 1 cup of cold water)
8 oz.	Tomato sauce (usually 1 can)
16 ozs.	Canned tomatoes – diced (usually 1 can)
	Enough water for proper texture

In a large sauté pan, brown meat (if raw). If you are using cooked meat, then sauté chopped onions and all peppers except the yellow bell peppers. Transfer to a chili pot and combine all ingredients, except the flour, over medium heat. It is at this point that you should add water to adjust the texture. The mixture should have sufficient water to cover the solid ingredients – this, however, is a matter of personal taste. After amount of water is adjusted, you should bring to a slight boil and lower heat to simmer, checking water content and stirring occasionally and adding water where necessary as contents reduce.

After mixture has simmered for enough time to tenderize the particular type of meat you have used, it is time to add the yellow bell pepper and the flour/water mixture to thicken the chili. The mixture should be returned to boil and simmered for about five minutes to cook the flour. Chili will then be ready to eat. This thickening process is not a necessary step, and can be omitted if desired.

Because this chili, like many other dishes, seems to improve after it has been refrigerated and reheated, we often double or triple the above recipe with much success. I wholeheartedly encourage you to experiment with this chili and change it to suit your taste and heat range. Be forewarned however, that as-is the above recipe is quite spicy and very hot.

CHAPTER THIRTEEN

SHRIMPING WITH COTTON

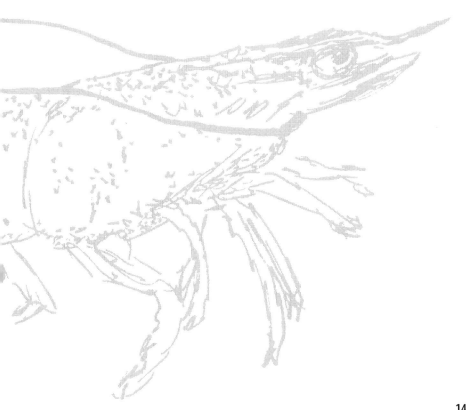

Shrimping with Cotton

It's 2:00 AM on a warm, humid summer morning. In the twilight of slumber, I faintly hear Cotton enter my room to awaken me for the day's work. Like most teenaged boys, I stayed out too late to have to be up at this time in the morning, but for some strange, primordial reason, I did it anyway. Knowing Cotton the way that any lad knows his dad (and thus fully realizing that excuses would be futile), I drag my sleep-deprived body up for another day's work on a shrimping vessel.

The quarry on our shrimping expeditions were either *Penaeus setiferus*, more commonly known as white shrimp; or *Penaeus aztecus*, also known as brown shrimp. In actuality, the two species are hardly discernible to the untrained eye, having only very subtle differences in physical characteristics and almost undetectable differences in taste. The two species do breed and gather in different areas at different times, and therefore we approached the harvest of them in different ways. Both species are varieties of prawn found along the Atlantic coast of North America and throughout the Gulf of Mexico. The largest of the species may reach a length of 7.8 inches, with the female being the larger of the two. The length of the antennae may reach up to three times such length. Both species of shrimp spawn in shallows of the open sea (at different times), with the hatchling returning to the estuaries to begin their growth cycles. After growing to a certain stage, the shrimp (both white and brown) will return to the open ocean to complete their life cycles. It was during such growth and migration cycles that the shrimp were harvested for food and commercial sales by my family.

Cotton had a 27 foot shrimp boat that, like all of the boats before this one, he built himself. His boat fell in a class of boats that were referred to as "inshore" boats, or boats that were shrimped primarily

Jim and Cotton on the shrimp boat

in the bays and inlets of the Texas-Louisiana coast, and usually within 25 miles of the coastline. During my teenage years, we lived in a small coastal town on a peninsula between the Gulf of Mexico and Galveston Bay. This gave us access to both the gulf and the bay for shrimping, crabbing and oystering, which were our primary activities for the family seafood business.

As usual, Cotton awakens me with all of the aplomb of a Marine drill Sargent or prison guard; the specific category being directly determined by how much sleep I had managed to get. He pours me a cup of hot coffee, and we talk while I mentally attempt to adjust the horizontal and vertical control knobs of my tired mind. It was during this conversation that Cotton would talk to me about what area of the bay he felt would be most productive for shrimping, and why. He would talk about the usual criteria such as tides, wind speed and direction and temperature, but he also used many unconventional indicators as well. Cotton always watched the phases of the moon, and paid a lot of attention to the birds and sea creatures that we encountered. The quantity of rain that had fallen usually indicated salinity changes in the bay, which in turn caused the shrimp to move, and where are the porpoise working? Cotton would feel the shells of the shrimp for firmness, and notice what type and quantity of small fish that were caught during shrimping. All of these things (and I guess many more that I have forgotten) all went into Cotton's decision as to where the shrimp were on a given day. He must have been pretty good at it, since his opinion was much-sought-after by the other shrimpers at the dock as we were departing for the day. Knowing this, and not wanting to give away his best shrimping spot, Cotton would often leave the dock and throw his net over (called making a "drag") in an alternate location. After the other fishermen would also put their nets out and begin dragging,

Cotton pulling in the net, circa 1982

we would slowly drag away from the pack, and when out of sight of them, we would pick up our net and go to the day's designated spot. Shrimping was a competitive business, so maneuvers of this type were commonplace; however, Cotton seemed to get a rather elfish pleasure out of fooling the other fishermen. As with many of man's earthly endeavors, there was an element of brinksmanship involved, which Cotton silently relished. Even though he spoke only in terms of the business competition, I knew that there was a more deep-seated, primordial motivation in the small games of deception on Cotton's part about where the best shrimp were on a given day. Cotton was known for catching shrimp when others did not, and he loved the feeling of satisfaction that came with that particular social sub current.

It's still twilight as the boat leaves the dock, crosses the Intracoastal Canal and enters Galveston Bay. As the boat heads out across the bay, the heavy, moist salt air blows through my hair. It's a smell and taste that haunts me to this day, and seems to constantly beckon me home. I watch Daddy as he scans the horizon with the eyes of a sage – a horizon that he has scanned many times over the years. What does he see? What subtle glimpses of nature's being does Cotton take in to guide him to a place where shrimp gather sufficient for a good catch on this day? As we glide over the water to our destination, Cotton makes adjustments to the net. He checks the metal strip along the bottom edge of the large wooden structures that cause the net to spread and stay open while dragging (called "doors") for wear. If the front edge of the metal strip is worn more than the back edge, then that is a sign for him to tighten up on the upper rope (or "cork line"), to pull the back end of the doors down so that they ride along the bottom. Conversely, if the back edge is worn more than the front edge, then he would loosen up a little on the cork line so that the wear was uniform along the metal edge. This was all done subconsciously with movements that were choreographed through time while Cotton was devoting his conscious energy toward finding shrimp for the day's catch. The sea birds are awakening, and they follow the boat knowing that a feast awaits them once we start

pulling in the nets and removing the small fish and other creatures that become their buffet. They screech with excitement as if to alert their friends that breakfast is on the way. Shortly after the net goes into the water and we begin dragging, the sun starts breaking on the horizon.

There is mysticism about daybreak on the water that has fascinated me for my entire life. The sun seems to rise up out of the water, and for a brief time, any clouds that are in the sky turn bright pink. Most of the time, there is little if any wind at sun rise, since the heat of the sun has something to do with the pressure variants that seem to cause winds. While we were dragging the net for the first time, Cotton would break out breakfast, since this was the only time we had available to eat. Once the net was picked up, there was constant work culling the catch and icing down the shrimp to get ready for the next time the net was pulled in. Our breakfast was various things that Cora would get up and prepare, but it was always good and there was always a lot of it since it was frequently the only thing we would have to eat until we finished at night. One of my favorites was an omelet sandwich made with crab meat and shrimp. Cora would wrap our sandwiches in waxed paper, then in foil, so that they would still be warm when we opened them up to eat. As I wander through the memories of my life, I can recall the smell and taste of the crab meat, shrimp and green onions sautéed in butter with an indescribable yearning that only a Cajun in his twilight years can understand.

The party's over – I hear the engine slow down and know that this is the signal to depart my mental dream state of being a wealthy industrialist, dining on delicate crab meat and shrimp and return to the world of the Cajun proletariat. The net is coming in, and I will now spend the rest of the day working with little (if any) break time. As the "doors" emerge from the water, the engine speeds up to bring the end of the net that holds the catch (called the "bag") to the surface. The bag is then hauled in, and the catch is dumped into the wooden enclosure used to cull the catch, appropriately named the "culling box." Once dumped, the culling box is teeming with sea life. The way that the net is made causes it to pick up everything that is in its path, therefore you have a very wide variety of creatures to pick through (some rather hazardous).

The job of culling the catch is not for the weak of heart. There is always something in the culling box that is trying to bite, sting, pinch or stick you. Part of the process of becoming a Cajun seems to involve being bitten, stung, pinched and stuck by all of these critters, and I suppose I succeeded somewhat in that regard. You do, however, develop a subconscious ability to navigate these dangers and get on to the business of culling the catch.

My job was to separate the shrimp from the catch, and then further separate them as to size before icing them down so that they stayed fresh. I would then clean and ice down any soft-shelled crabs and regular crabs, in addition to any fish that were marketable, such as flounder, speckled trout and redfish. This pretty much made up our catch in the bay. On those times when we ventured out of the bay into the gulf (or "off shore" as it is referred), you could add to that list any number of other fish types that were marketable; however, the bay catch made up the bulk of our market. On the last drag, I would usually keep 6 to 8 of the very large, encrusted blue crabs for Cora to boil for me as I was cleaning out the nets and preparing the boat for the next day's trip. This was always one of my favorite treats of the day – a boiled crab appetizer before I ate a big bowl of Cora's shrimp and crab stew.

Cora's Boiled Shrimp

Boiled shrimp are, by every outward appearance, one of the most basic of all Cajun foods. When I was growing up, Mama would serve boiled shrimp as one would serve a salad prior to eating the main course but occasionally, boiled shrimp would be the main meal. Mostly served hot but occasionally cold, boiled shrimp were eaten frequently, especially during the late spring through late fall when shrimp were being caught. Mama always said that shrimp that were boiled without the heads left on did not taste right; therefore, we seldom had boiled shrimp during the winter months. I can never remember eating shrimp boiled without the heads, or crabs boiled that had been cleaned, because Cora said that the water was flavored by the heads of shrimp and the parts of the crab that you disposed of when you cleaned crabs. She felt that the water would become a seafood stock, and without it, the boiled seafood would just not be correct. When we did have shrimp off-season, it was only because Mama had frozen some with the heads on immersed in water, stored in the waxed paper milk cartons that milk used to come in prior to the plasticized paper cartons that are common today. Freezing shrimp with the heads on will only work successfully if they are frozen while very freshly caught in a block of ice, with no exposure to the air. They then must be completely thawed out while floating in cool water to maintain the integrity of the heads in preparation for boiling. This may seem like a lot of trouble, but this method will ensure that the shrimp taste as close to freshly-caught as possible. Cora and Cotton both always felt and said that the most important part of any seafood dish was how the seafood was handled and cared for prior to any type of preparation.

Cora's boiled shrimp were rather tame when compared to the boiled shrimp of today. The reason for this is the profusion of spices and spice mixes that are commercially-available, coupled with the mistaken impression that all Cajun food must be over-the-top spicy to be truly authentic. In actuality, when I was very young, the only boiling spice that was available was the dry packaged crab boil mix of spices in the small cloth bag. There are currently many different spice combinations and preparations available that all claim to be authentically Cajun, the most notorious of which are the boiling powders. I can only imagine what my Mama would have said to me if I had brought home crab boil in powder form for her to use. Since disposable income (or lack thereof) was a constant problem for most bayou Cajuns, purchasing the packaged crab boil mix was a little bit of a luxury. Mama even talked about actually making the crab boil mix she used when she was younger and "when money was tight yeah."

Fortunately, I had Mama write down the recipe she used for home-made crab boil mix. Many of the ingredients used were grown, dried and saved from her garden. She traded for the rest at the general store. The list of ingredients went something like this: 4 tablespoons of mustard seeds; 2 tablespoons each of celery seeds, black peppercorns, dill seeds; 3 tablespoons of coriander seeds; 2 tablespoons of whole allspice (when she could get it); 1 tablespoon of whole cloves; 8 to 10 laurel (bay) leaves; several thyme leaves and 2 or 3 dried cayenne peppers split long-ways. Mama said that you could boil about 5 pounds of shrimp with this much seasoning, or about three dozen crabs. I actually gathered up the ingredients and made this boiling mixture myself, and despite the trouble of locating and acquiring everything to make it, I was surprised at how good it turned out.

I can still remember watching Mama boil shrimp in the tiny kitchen of our home. It was a pretty frequent sight, since we caught shrimp every day, and for us it was free food. To boil shrimp, Mama would take a large stock pot that she called her boiling pot (imagine that), and bring about two gallons of salted water to a boil. Mama would never measure the salt, but would add salt until the water tasted right – she said it should taste about like the ocean. On occasion, when she wanted to spice up the shrimp, Mama would add a dried cayenne pepper or two that she had saved from her garden, or a couple of bird's eye peppers she had growing by the back door, to the boiling water. She would then add a box of dry crab boil mix after tearing open the cloth sack to let the seasonings be loose in the water. Although this might seem rather uncivilized, I am sure that this reminded her of when they made their own boiling mixture. To this day, I tear open the cloth bags to boil my seafood. I love the look of the seasonings mixed with the boiled shrimp, and the occasional burst of flavor you get when some of the spices themselves get eaten with the shrimp.

After the seasonings, Cora would pour a tablespoon or so of olive oil in the water, which she said would make the shrimp peel easier. Then, she would add cut up lemons, red potatoes and sometimes smoked sausage, and boil them until the potatoes would be almost done (could be slightly pierced with a fork). At this point, she would tear open another bag of crab boil mixture into the pot and add several ribs of celery, corn on the cob, about five pounds of shrimp, and occasionally 2 to 4 bottles of beer. Cora would boil the shrimp for about 8 to 10 minutes, depending upon the size of the shrimp. Larger shrimp have to be boiled a little longer; smaller shrimp, a little less.

The ritual I have just described was carried out several times a week when I was growing up. When Mama was boiling shrimp to accompany other dishes, she would usually leave out the corn and potatoes (and sausage). When Cora was boiling shrimp for a get-together, or when family was coming, it was done out in the yard with the wood fire and the three-legged cast iron pot. The recipe actually did not change much, with the exception of being

Aigrette

scaled up for the pot size. Since boiled seafood was part of a social event for Cajuns, oftentimes shrimp, crabs and crawfish were boiled; sometimes all together. I can still remember the conversations at these meetings, where the old folks would talk of past events and adventures that occurred while hunting and fishing on the bayous and estuaries that made up our neighborhood. Cora was especially adept at story-telling, and could keep children mesmerized for hours with tales of her father as a trapper in southern Louisiana. One particular tale was about a time when my grandfather was stalked by a large black cat for months while he ran his traps in the bayous. The story never seemed to have an end, but Mama would tell different parts of the event through the eyes of an observer, all with an exceptional eye for detail. She would talk of the beauty of the swamp and the *aigrette* (pronounced *a grett'*, meaning egret) nesting in the moss-draped cypress along the bayou's edge. I can still remember holding my breath as Mama recalled the sound of the cat breathing as my grandfather past under a tree limb that the great cat was perched upon. Cora was sort of a pragmatic romantic, if there is such a thing; an intellectual person who was scarcely educated, caught in a time warp. I often feel that Mama was the reincarnation of bits and pieces of a long series of individuals like Henry Thoreau, Harriet Beecher Stowe, Samuel Taylor Coleridge and Rosa Parks.

Over the years, I have continued to boil shrimp in Mama's tradition; however, I have modernized the recipe somewhat with the addition of liquid crab boil mix. This suits the tastes of the New Orleans lady I am married to, who likes things a little more on the spicy side. The following recipe works quite well for today's tastes, but remains essentially true to Mama's original recipe for boiled shrimp.

Boiled Shrimp

INGREDIENTS:

8 quarts	Water
2 boxes	Dry crab boil mix *(3 oz.)*
4 oz.	Bottle of liquid crab boil
1 tbsp.	Olive oil
¼-⅓ cup	Salt *(to taste, but should be somewhat salty)*
2-4	Bottles of beer
2	Lemons, whole
4 stems	Celery *(washed and halved)*
4 ears	Corn *(shucked and halved – can use frozen half ears)*
3-4 lbs.	Small red potatoes *(skins on/washed and brushed)*
5-7 lbs.	Shrimp *(head-on)*
Optional:	
1	Dried cayenne pepper – split long ways

In a large stock pot (16 qt. or larger), combine the water, liquid crab boil, salt (one dried cayenne pepper) and one box of dry crab boil (with the mesh bag torn open) and bring to a boil. Add red potatoes and boil until fork tender. When potatoes are done, remove them from boiling water and place in a bowl covered with a towel to keep them warm.

To the boiling water, add olive oil and the other box of dry crab boil mix, and re-salt* if desired, since the potatoes will absorb some of the salt. Add celery, corn, shrimp and beer. Cut lemons in half, squeeze juice in boiling water, and drop halves in the water. Return mixture to boil and continue boiling for 8 to 10 minutes, depending upon the size of the shrimp. Remember that you can remove and peel a shrimp at different points during boiling to test for desired doneness. My preference when boiling shrimp is to boil them until there is a slight visual separation of the shell from the meat for ease of peeling. Others do not like to boil shrimp quite to this stage, so there is an element of personal judgment involved with the timing of boiling shrimp. After a couple of times, you will be able to determine your preference – the right way is whichever way you like. Remove vegetables and shrimp from boiling water (after "soaking"), and serve shrimp hot with Dodie's red sauce. Serve the potatoes and corn with butter.

RE: Soaking – Once the shrimp or crabs are boiled for the proper time period, Creole Cajuns like to turn the fire off and let the seafood "soak" for a up to five minutes. The theory (a word not often used when talking about Cajuns) here is that the seafood will absorb the seasonings. The jury (a word that is often used when referring to Cajuns) is still out as to whether the seafood absorbs more seasonings, but the seafood does seem to get saltier.

A note about salt – the potatoes absorb quite a bit of salt, but since there can be health issues with the use of salt, discretion comes into play at this point. If you do elect to re-salt, then never use more than ½ the amount you originally chose to use. Traditional Cajun seafood boiling is very salty but then again, Cajun food never claimed to be health food.

Dodie's Red Sauce

When you are eating the boiled shrimp, every good Cajun knows that you need a good red sauce and my Creole Cajun, New Orleans born wife, Dodie (a Cajun nickname for Dorothy), makes the best red sauce I have ever tasted. Its simplicity is probably its most striking feature.

INGREDIENTS:

  12 oz. Ketchup (about ½ a bottle)
1-2 tbsp. Prepared horseradish (or 3 or 4)
  1 tbsp. Lime juice (to taste)

This is a simple recipe that Dodie came up with that works exquisitely with boiled or fried seafood dishes. She does not really measure these ingredients, but makes adjustments to taste and it always comes out well. We like it very hot, so she leans more toward adding a lot of horseradish. After you make this a couple of times, you will quickly learn your preferences.

157

Dried Shrimp

Long before there was refrigeration as a means of keeping shrimp from spoiling, shrimp were dried as a way to have them available year round. Like many Cajuns before her, Mama dried shrimp for her family. Even though we had a refrigerator and a freezer, Cora continued to dry shrimp because it comforted her to maintain links to the past. Cora often waxed poetic about her childhood, as if the marsh were an idyllic setting. As I reflect on my life growing up in the salt marshes and sea cane, it does now seem idyllic in a strange sort of way.

Cora grew up with dried shrimp used in gumbos and stews, not to mention using them as a unique snack food. I can still remember the salty taste of Mama's dried shrimp when I would sneak out to the back porch, where Mama stored all of our canned vegetables and preserved provisions, and sneak a handful from the large jar where they were stored. The dried shrimp tasted and smelled of the sea, and when I eat them now, I can remember playing out in the yard while I ate dried shrimp. Occassionally, I will make a gumbo with dried shrimp to remind me of Mama and growing up. Although I am probably the only Cajun you will ever meet who does not favor okra in my gumbos and stews, I always add okra to a gumbo made with dried shrimp, because Mama always said the okra gumbo made with dried shrimp was her favorite. I loved Mama.

Making dried shrimp was a process that I did many times with Mama. Daddy had made for Mama two large drying frames with screen on one side, similar to a screen door but not quite as wide. The reason the width was critical was the fact that the drying frames had to be brought into the house at night to prevent the higher moisture of the night from causing any bacterial growth to start. When drying shrimp, the first frame was placed on sawhorses outside in the sun with the screen side down. After the shrimp were placed on the first frame to dry, the other frame was placed on top of the first frame, this time with the screen side up. This allowed the shrimp to be completely encased in a compartment with high air flow that prevented flies and other insects from making contact with the shrimp that were drying. This was a pretty ingenious way to get the job done. Cotton made two sets of these drying frames for Cora which would allow us to dry about 40 to 50 pounds of shrimp each time. Cotton was a gifted inventor, and when Cora wanted something to help her perform some sort of task, Cotton would create a device that would work divinely. The symbiosis that existed in and around Mama and Daddy was warming to all who knew them.

Drying shrimp with Mama always started with her telling Daddy that she wanted about 50 pounds of very fresh shrimp. The size was usually not that important, but Mama liked to dry larger shrimp (since they were easier to remove from the shells after drying). Mama insisted on the freshest shrimp possible, since it was her contention that if you were going to expend the effort to preserve food, you should always start with the freshest and best to increase the chances that your finished product would be good. Into her boiling pot Mama would put barely enough water to cover the shrimp, and she would add about twice the amount of salt she would use for boiling shrimp. Unlike boiling shrimp, she would start with the shrimp in cold water over medium heat, and would slowly bring the shrimp to a boil, and then continue to boil for about 15 minutes, stiring occasionally. She would them turn off the heat and let the shrimp totally cool off while still in the salted water. She said the reason for this was for the shrimp to absorb as much salt as possible, because salt was the preservative.

Once they had cooled, the shrimp were placed in a single layer on the first drying frame (screen side down). The top frame was placed with screen side up on top of the first frame, and they were allowed to sit in the full sun for no less than three days (bringing them in at night).

By the time the shrimp had completely dried, the heads were probably so dry that they were crumbling to dust, so whatever of the shell and heads that can be removed should be. The dried shrimp were then placed in a pillow case and hung up on the clothes-line out in the sun. Mama would send us out to "fluff" up the pillow case to continue breaking up the shells of the dried shrimp. After a day or two of this, we would sit down and separate the dried shrimp from the shell and put the dried shrimp into large glass jars with tight lids. If done correctly, dried shrimp would keep for a long period of time.

Cora's Boiled Crabs

When a bunch of Cajuns decide to get together, regardless of the reason, you can bet that there will be beer and (depending upon the season) boiled crawfish or crabs. Since crabs were available in our region for a much longer season, they played a much more prominent role in our social settings. Like boiled crawfish, boiled crabs were often the food of choice for social events, and were never meant to actually serve as a complete meal. When Cajuns would sit down to a table of boiled crabs, there was ample time to discuss the events of the day. It was a time to catch up on what was happening in everyone's lives, and to reflect on events of the world outside of the bayou that came to Cajuns in fragmented segments. My Uncle George would

occasionally buy a copy of the Port Arthur News, a newspaper of a small city where he and Cotton sometimes went to sell seafood. The occasional newspaper and a rather large Stromberg Carlson radio that Uncle George owned were our only sources of what was going on in the outside world.

By the time I was born, the roads that led you to and from Sabine Pass, Texas were paved and actually pretty good. Cotton often spoke of the poor condition of the roads in the 1930's, back in the earlier days of the automobile. He told me that the roads were so bad that the trip to Port Arthur from Sabine Pass (about 13 miles) usually took all day, and often involved getting stuck in the mud several times, or contending with mechanical break-downs. Because of such difficulties, "trips to town" as they were referred were only made when you needed to sell some seafood combined, with securing needed parts, etc. Even after the roads improved in the late 40's, "goin' to town" was still rare and was treated as a combined trip for necessities that could only be gotten there.

The outside world and its happenings were all the more tantalizing, and often dominated the conversation around the table while eating boiled crabs. Peeling and eating boiled crabs is a rather labor-intensive process. This made eating boiled crabs a perfect social event for Cajuns. As the night wore on, the conversation changed from outside world events to segments of daily struggle. Ultimately, the conversation finally came to personal strife. It was during this part of the evening that Cajuns shared the part of life that they had in common with the rest of humanity, and that was the daily struggle of dealing with life and existence. Like the rest of the world, Cajuns actually had no idea that they were virtually the same as all the other peoples of the world. All nationalities and ethnicities have the uninformed impression that their strife and struggles with existence are unique, but sadly they are not. Perhaps it is better that they did not know this then, and probably do not know it now.

Boiling crabs Cajun-style is very similar to the way that they boil shrimp. The main differences are the size of the pot and the proportions of the seasonings. Almost every day on the shrimp boat, I would keep about 8 very large crabs from the last drag. When we arrived back at the house, I would give Mama the crabs, and she would "put them on to boil," as she would say. By the time that I had finished cleaning up the boat and had hung the nets up to dry, the crabs would be finished and waiting for me. The boiled crabs were a great appetizer for whatever meal that Mama had prepared. Even though I was not aware of it at the time, being able to sit down to fresh boiled crabs virtually every day was a luxury of immeasurable proportions. I guess it is normal for people to take for granted that which is common to them. It is only when something which they frequently had available is no longer there that they can take the time to realize its true value. I have Mama's crab boiling recipe, and it goes like this:

Cora's Boiled Crabs

INGREDIENTS:

8-10 qts.	Water
2 boxes	Dry crab boil mix (3 oz.)
4 oz.	Bottle of liquid crab boil
1 tbsp.	Olive oil
¼-⅓ c.	Salt (to taste, but should be somewhat salty)
2	Lemons (whole)
4 stems	Celery (washed and halved)
4 ears	Corn (shucked and halved – can use frozen half ears)
3-4 lbs.	Small red potatoes (skins on/washed and brushed)
18-24	Whole live crabs

Optional:

1	Dried cayenne pepper, split long ways
2-4	Bottles of beer

In a large stock pot (16 qt. or larger), combine the water, liquid crab boil, salt, dried cayenne pepper (if using) and one box of dry crab boil with the mesh bag torn open, and bring to a boil. Add red potatoes and boil until fork tender. When potatoes are done, remove them from boiling water and place in a bowl covered with a towel to keep them warm.

To the boiling water, add the other box of dry crab boil mix and re-salt if desired since the potatoes will absorb some of the salt. Add crabs, beer (if you elect to use it), celery and corn. Cut lemons in half, squeeze juice in boiling water, and drop halves in the water. Return mixture to boil and continue boiling 10 minutes. Remove vegetables and crabs from boiling water and serve. Serve the potatoes and corn with butter. When served as an appetizer, allow 2 to 4 crabs per person (6 to 8 crabs per Cajun). If you intend to make a social event out of crab boiling, then you should double these quantities and ice down a lot of beer.

CHAPTER FOURTEEN

OYSTERING

Oystering

It's about three o'clock in the morning, and I really do not feel like getting up. No kid in his mid-teens ever wants to be up at this time of the day doing anything, much less going out on a wet, cold morning to toil all day performing back-breaking labor. Well, that is precisely what is about to happen. I pretend to be asleep, hoping Cotton will forget about taking me oystering and let me sleep. Rats! It does not work – even though I have tried it many times, and it never does. He wakes me up anyway.

I arise to the smell of strong coffee and breakfast being prepared by Cora, who gives the appearance of having been up for hours. Coffee is on the table for me, while Cotton is on probably what is his third or fourth cup. Cheerful to a fault, Cora packs breakfast for Cotton and I, and we are off. Everything on the oyster boat is cold and wet because, after all, it is winter time. As Galveston bay water gets colder, the oysters get fatter and develop a rich taste to behold. The boat engine finally warms up to operating temperature, and we leave the dock for the open waters of the bay. Although they smell fresh and clean, the cold winter winds seem to cut you like a knife as the oyster boat glides across the bay waters. The tears streaming down your face caused by the sharp winds seem to freeze on your skin. Just when you decide you can't take the cold wind any longer, you reach the oyster beds and the long slow grind of the oyster dredge brings a constant flow of work.

An oyster dredge is a hellish device constructed out of a heavy steel frame, with steel teeth that dig and tear at the oysters that grow on the reefs of Galveston bay. As the oyster clusters are loosened from the sea bed, they slide past the mouth of the dredge and are held in a chain-link bag attached to the back of the dredge. There is so much damage and wear to the dredge that bent, broken and worn down teeth are constantly being repaired or replaced. The bag of the oyster dredge holds about two bushels of oysters, loose and in clusters, along with an assortment of other things that are part of the oyster bed on the floor of the bay. As bad as the dredge sounds, it is light years ahead of our earlier method of harvesting oysters with oyster tongs. Oyster tongs consists of what appear to be two very long-handled (ten to twelve feet) garden rakes that are hinged so that they close up and grab large clusters of oysters. that are then hauled up from the bay floor and hoisted onto the deck of a boat to be culled for usable oysters. The weight of a large cluster of oysters coupled with the weight of tongs made this an exhaustive process. Tongin' for oysters was a tough way to make a living, and made the oyster dredge look pretty good. The dredge is pulled in and dumped at regular intervals, usually every minute or two, precipitating constant back-breaking labor on the part of the deck crew which in this case was me.

The oysters that were the subject of our adventure were primarily the Eastern oyster *Cassostrea Virginica*, a very common shellfish having two tightly-fitting shells joined at one end by a hinge joint, and firmly held in place by the adductor muscle that is attached to each shell at the dark oval (clearly visible when the shells do not have oysters in them). The Eastern oyster can grow to be quite large, up to 8 inches in length, and are known by several other names such as Texas oysters probably due to their large size and coon oysters since raccoons were very fond of eating oysters when they had access during the occasional extreme low tides of winter. Another variety of oyster (though not as common) that we harvested was a more regularly-shaped oyster known as the "cup" oyster, or as Cotton referred to them, "Houma" oysters. Houma oysters were the darling of the oyster bar set since their regular shape and compact size rendered them perfect for half-shell consumption. The interior of the shell also had rose colored overtones which gave them more eye appeal.

Oysters have the ability to change sex from male to female when environmental circumstances necessitate such changes, presumably without suffering any societal ramifications. Oysters reproduce by spewing their eggs and sperm into the water, where the eggs are fertilized, and land upon other oysters or empty shells to begin forming their own shells for their circle of life. At this stage in their life, the young oysters are referred to as "spats." When the water temperature begins to drop in the late fall and early winter, oysters begin storing a flavor-enhancing carbohydrate compound within their bodies called glycogen. By the time that the bay waters are at their coldest, usually the months from January up to March, oysters are at their fattest and sweetest, and have become the ultimate flavor experience (to an oyster lover). It was only during this time that we would freeze the oysters that we would personally eat for the coming year.

Because oysters have to attach themselves to something hard, (usually another oyster shell) to begin their life cycle, they ultimately grow in large clusters. These clusters have to be broken apart into single oysters in a process called "culling," using a striking device called an "oyster hatchet." The culled oysters are tossed into heavy wire, bushel baskets with no bottom, which are placed into the mouth of a burlap sack. When the basket is full of culled oysters, you grab the edges of the sack and lift the basket, allowing the oysters to fall into the sack, thereby having a measured bushel of oysters sacked and ready to sell. Although Cotton did not sell his oysters "by the sack" as it was referred, we followed this same process as a means to measure the yield of our oystering adventure, which usually became the topic of conversation with the other oyster fishermen over coffee. As with shrimping, Cotton was one of the more adept of the fishermen, and our oyster catch, per trip, was usually on the high end of the catches.

When I was very young, in conversations with Mama, I would ask her how Daddy knew where the shrimp, crabs or oysters where on a given day. Did he "taste the water" or "smell them in the air?" Mama said that she did not know, but that Cotton was a good man who always did a good job at anything he did, because he tried harder than anybody else did. Although that answer did not seem like it made any sense to me at the time, it became clearer as I began to grow older. Actually, Cotton always seemed to know where a successful catch was because he was attentive to all things. Cotton's mind was always on duty, observing the sky, wind, the action of the sea birds, cloud formations (especially at daybreak and at dusk), barometric pressure and the cycles of the moon. In addition to atmospheric conditions, he watched the firmness of the shells of the shrimp, how fat the fish were in the net, the taste of the raw oysters on a given oyster bed at a given time, how the shells appeared on crabs, and other things that all went together to form a lifetime of understanding of the sea that only Cotton could decipher. The sum of all of Cotton's parts equaled the ultimate Cajun fisherman.

When the oyster boat finally arrived at the dock, all of the sacks of oysters had to be unloaded and kept dry and cool until they were opened and the oysters were washed and packaged for selling. Since we oystered predominately in the winter, keeping the oysters cool was not a problem. Keeping oysters dry meant that you did not want them to get water poured over them, at least until you were ready to open them immediately, since when they sensed water, they could open up and the water that they were holding in their shells could run out. An oyster holds a quantity of water in its shell to hold it over until the tide comes back in, since oysters can and do grow in tidal areas where they can be out of the water for some time. When the time came for opening the oysters (or "shucking"), the sacks were moved from the holding room into the opening area for removal and processing.

The holding and opening rooms for the oysters consisted of basically a two room building that was built by Cotton and me out of salvaged lumber that we collected after being washed up on the beach. I can still remember Cotton driving down the beach, pulling the trailer behind his truck as I walked alongside picking up usable boards on the beach. During the 1950's, the maritime laws were not as strict about throwing things into the water, and there was a considerable amount of lumber tossed into the sea by ships leaving the Port of Galveston which was used as dunnage for stacking and storing cargo. There was also a large amount of timber from shipwrecks and storms which struck the Gulf of Mexico with some degree of frequency. As I was picking up lumber, my mind used to wander about where these boards came from, and what their story was. Many of the boards were of a wood species not found in our area, or in North America for that matter. Where did the tree grow that produced this board, and who had cut it down? When we would saw the boards, they smelled different and exotic, as if they were from a distant land. Other boards were joined together, and would be part of a wall or section of a shipwreck that had to be dismantled to get the usable pieces of lumber. Cotton would get out to help me load those pieces. These pieces, often painted and finished, seemed to try and tell their story to you in bits and pieces. I used to imagine a crew at sea, fighting the storm for their very lives. Did they survive, or did they arrive at a fate that I and all fishermen think about in the back of their minds; the time when you lose your battle for survival and become a bit player in the endless drama of the sea. Other boards that were on the beach told no story at all and seemed to be out-of-place, like they should not be there.

When Cotton pulled the trailer up beside our house, the real work of pulling the nails out of the boards and sorting them began. After a time, when a certain amount of lumber had been accumulated, Cotton and I would begin the process of erecting some sort of structure that Cotton had designed in his mind, based upon the lumber we had on hand. In this case, it was a holding area and opening area for our oystering activities. These two rooms were basic in their design and construction, with wooden walls and floor and a corrugated metal roof. Boards that had been previously painted were randomly placed next to unpainted boards, giving the place a patchwork look but (like typical Cajun structures), they we structurally sound and usable. Because we oystered in the winter (when there were no shrimp to catch and crabs were scarce), the opening room was heated with an old wood burning stove for which Cotton traded something to somebody at some point – who knows. And as you probably have guessed, we burned the leftover scraps from construction in the stove to keep warm. Cajuns, like so many socio-economically disadvantaged ethnic cultures, were the original recyclers, using every last crumb of something until all traces of it are gone.

The opening and processing phases of the oystering cycle was the part that I suppose I remember the most, since it involved Cotton, Cora and I sitting across from each other, conversing as we worked at a lengthy, monotonous job. As you open oysters, you get into a rhythm that allows a duality of existence. This only comes after you have stuck your hand a couple of times with your oyster knife, and have learned by trial and error the best places to enter the oyster shell for optimum speed of opening. After you become a veteran of minor (hopefully) injuries and you have mastered the skill of efficient opening, it all becomes rather autonomic, and you have the mental space for other things. As I am writing, I can remember the smell of the burning wood in the old stove where we would stop occasionally to warm our hands. Cora would often put a pot of hot chocolate on for me, and Cotton always had coffee ready. Cora would always simmer things on the wood stove like soups and stocks since it was "hot anyway" and it was "no use to waste the heat." The most memorable part was the conversations I had with Cotton and Cora. Mama would tell me stories from her past that were rich in detail, and Daddy would explain how to do things, how to make things, how things worked and other bits of knowledge. It's sad that the profusion of knowledge provided by one's parents is dispensed during the drama of searching for one's self during one's teenage years, but somehow, I guess it all works out.

Cora would be the one to take over when the oysters were opened and ready for processing. She would lightly wash the oysters on a large straining table, and loosely pack them in gallon tins that were topped off with a couple cups of rain water which had been cooled with ice. Cotton was a firm believer in rain water, and that was all we drank growing up. Living on the coast with frequent rains gave us an abundance of rainwater caught off of the roof in a large metal tank called a cistern. Cotton would place a cloth bag filled with charcoal over the incoming spout to the cistern, and we always had plenty of fresh rainwater to drink. The tins filled with oysters were then placed in a refrigerator to await delivery to our customers. During this holding time of one to two days, the oysters would re-hydrate themselves and be fat and ready to eat. Everyone said that Cotton's oysters were the very best, and most people would only get their oysters from Cotton.

Fried Oysters

Ah – one of my favorites. Mama would fry a mountain of oysters for us to eat, and eat them we did. For all of you who have not yet tried oysters, this is the first dish with oysters that you probably should try. This will teach you to like oysters enough to move on to dishes where the oyster flavor can be somewhat overpowering to the uninitiated palate. Oysters are definitely a finalist for what word goes into the blank in "the bravest man in the world was the first man to

Jim and oyster buddy Ed at a recent oyster feast

eat _____." They are soft and wet, and only have a taste reminiscent of the fresh sea breezes to the most ardent of oyster lovers. Eating oysters is a learned experience, but developing a taste for them is certainly rewarding in the end. I recommend frying them until they are very well done (or as a Cajun would say, frying them until they are "hard") when eating them for the first time, then gradually cooking them "softer," or for a shorter cooking period, until you reach the point where you are most satisfied. This is how I taught my wife to eat oysters since she had not acquired a taste for them prior to our marriage. Prior to meeting my wife, it was always rather hard for me to relate to someone not having a taste for oysters, because they were always in our household since we were in the business. I do not remember eating them for the first time.

When frying Cajun style, there are a few points to remember. Once again, cast iron is the pot of choice, since it holds heat well, and a high temperature oil like vegetable oil is required. Bacon grease and a hydrogenated oil or shortening were the oils of choice when I was young; however, vegetable oil came into use and canola oil is now widely available, and it is really a better alternative. Be sure to use enough oil as my Daddy would say, "to float da oysters," and for uniform cooking and heat retention. Don't overload the skillet since you do not want to significantly reduce the heat at any given point in the cooking process, or the food will be too greasy.

INGREDIENTS:
    1 qt.   Oysters
    1 can   Evaporated milk
    1 lb.   Coarse ground corn meal *(stone ground is si bon)*
    1 qt.   Vegetable oil *(canola is preferable) – amount may vary depending upon type of vessel used*
            Salt to taste
            Cayenne pepper to taste

About one hour before you plan to begin cooking, pour oysters in a bowl and wash them in their own liquid (individually), so that incidental pieces of shell are removed. As you wash each one, place them in a bowl containing the evaporated milk. I like to add the cayenne pepper to the evaporated milk and stir it well before I add in the oysters. When all of the oysters have been added, place the bowl in the refrigerator for about ½ hour prior to cooking.

Select a cooking vessel that is about four inches deep (or deeper) like a cast iron, dutch oven bottom so that you can pour in at least two inches of oil and still have sufficient height left to contain the bubbling oil during frying.

Begin heating the oil over high heat until a temperature of about 360 deg. F is attained. I would highly recommend using a frying thermometer for accuracy. While the oil is heating, pour the cornmeal into a large baking pan (I use a 9" X 13"). Remove the oysters from the refrigerator and begin battering them in preparation to frying. Using the "wet hand/dry hand" method, remove an oyster with your wet hand and coat it thoroughly with cornmeal with the dry hand, until you have enough battered to load your cooking vessel. Once you have put the first load into the oil, you can begin battering the next batch to go into the hot oil. It's also important to remember that in order to maintain the proper cooking temperature, you have to have some battered oysters ready to immediately put in when you take the cooked oysters out. Turn the oysters after the bottom and edges start to lightly brown. As you take the oysters out of the oil, place them on newspaper covered with paper towels to absorb the excess oil and salt to taste while they are still very hot.

If strict authenticity is not a concern with you, then you can avoid a lot of your frying concerns by going to your local "big box" and buying an electric deep fryer with a temperature control on it. Then all you have to do is "set it and forget it." Your oysters will probably turn out just fine.

Cora's Chicken and Oyster Gumbo

Poulet (pronounced *poole let'*, meaning chicken) and oyster gumbo was one of my Daddy's favorites. As soon as the water temperature started to drop in the early winter, Cotton would start to talk about making a chicken and oyster gumbo. This, of course, coincided with the end of catching shrimp in the mid to late fall. We preferred to eat oysters when the water temperature was cooler, since the flavor of oysters improves a lot during the cooler months of winter and early spring. I can still remember seeing Cotton eat an oyster to test for the right time for chicken and oyster gumbo. The old adage that said that "you are only supposed to eat oysters in months with an 'r' in them" has some logical support. Months with an "r" in them are the months from September thru April, which are also the months associated with cooling and colder temperatures including water temperature. Cotton always held that the flavor of oysters improves when the water temperature drops, and after a lifetime of eating oysters, I am inclined to agree with that premise. To this day, I almost always get my oysters, in the shell, during the months of February or March when the water temperature is at its lowest. Because I became skilled at opening oysters in my

Poulet

youth, I prefer to eat oysters that I open myself, since there is a certain amount of subjectivity regarding the quality of oysters as they are being opened. I only keep the oysters that are "full and fat," with a complete complement of oyster liquor in the shell.

Cotton was always particular about the way we handled our oysters in the shell prior to opening them. He never let us drop the sacks of oysters when we were unloading the boat, preferring that the sack be set down gently. Oysters are immersed in a liquid, which is a combination of water and other secretions, that they need to survive. This liquid is referred to as their "liquor," or "oyster liquor.": When oysters are handled roughly while in the shell, their shells can get chipped on the edges, and their liquor can run out. Cotton also kept the sacks of oysters to be opened as cool as he could, but the colder temperatures of the winter months usually helped in that regard. He also kept the sacks of oysters in the shells as dry as possible, and never rinsed them off until it was immediately time for shucking. Oysters are tidal creatures that are occasionally out of water during low tide. During that time, oysters will tightly close their shells and re-circulate their liquor to keep themselves alive until the tide comes back in and they are again immersed in water. If you get oysters wet during storage prior to opening, they might sense the water and think that the tide is coming in, and open their shells causing the liquor to run out. These are just some of the components of my Mama and Daddy's belief that handling and caring for seafood prior to cooking is equally important as the recipe or preparation.

Oh, the smell of Mama's roux when this dish was being prepared is such a strong memory of my childhood. Every time I cook this or any recipe with roux, I can see Mama in her tiny kitchen stirring gumbo.

INGREDIENTS:

1 pint	Roux
5 qts.	Water

The Mirepoix:

3	Large yellow onions
4 cups	Coarsely chopped celery
2	Large coarsely chopped green bell pepper
1	Whole chicken cut up in pieces
1 qt.	Oysters
1 cup	Chopped green onions
½ cup	Chopped fresh parsley
1	Dozen eggs
5	Teaspoons of sea salt (or to taste)
	Filé to taste

Optional:

2-4	Chopped jalapenos *(not exactly Cajun but tasty)*, or:
1-2 tsps.	Cayenne pepper *(very Cajun)*

Coarsely chop 2 of your 3 large yellow onions (reserve one onion for later), and combine with vegetable oil, celery and bell pepper (mirepoix) and type of pepper (if desired) in a large stockpot over medium-high heat for a light sauté. Add water and bring to a rolling boil. Remove metal lid from the jar of roux and microwave for about 2 to 3 minutes until roux is warmed (warming the roux makes it melt and combine with the water quicker). Spoon roux into the boiling water, stirring continuously, until all of the roux is completely melted. If excess foaming occurs that cannot be controlled by continuously stirring, lower heat and continue until all roux is dissolved. Add one piece of chicken and three or four oysters to flavor the mixture. After roux mixture has simmered for about one hour, add in chicken pieces, and after returning to a boil, lower heat and simmer for about 30 to 45 minutes to cook chicken, stirring occasionally. The liquid will reduce somewhat, but when the oysters are added, they will release some liquid back into the dish.

Boil one dozen eggs in a sauce pan until hard boiled. Crack and peel eggs, and reserve for later use when serving gumbo.

After simmering, the heat should be elevated to return the mixture to a boil. The yellow onion that was reserved should be cut up in slices, separated into rings and dropped into the mixture for appearance and texture. You can additionally add a chopped red, yellow or orange bell pepper at this point. Drain oysters and add to gumbo, and lower heat to maintain low boil and to cook oysters for 5 to 10 minutes. Then, turn off heat and stir parsley and green onions into the mixture. Serve over cooked rice with filé and one or two peeled, hard boiled eggs.

A word about use of the oyster liquor: When cooking any oyster dish, Cajun cooking usually calls for straining the oyster liquor (to remove any shell pieces that might be present) and adding it into the dish for a more complete oyster flavor signature to the specific dish. Well-developed oyster lovers will welcome this addition to the dish, but new-comers to oyster consumption might consider this a bit overpowering, so care should be taken when considering such use of the oyster liquor.

Smoked Oysters

When I cook outside, I use one of my Daddy's tricks, and that was using sassafras wood for the unique smoked flavor it gives to meat (especially most seafood, chicken and pork), cooked over the glowing embers of a hardwood fire or (as is usually the case nowadays) lump charcoal embers. Cotton rarely used charcoal when he cooked out on his outdoor cooker, which was a home-made grill welded from an oil drum that he had acquired. After he had cut the drum to shape with a metal cutting torch and welded the parts that held the two cast iron grills that he had scavenged from heavens-knows-where, Cotton would then fill the cavity of the drum with hardwood, opening the top and bottom vents to let in maximum air and set the wood afire. The large amount of wood would burn for some time, and then the embers would smolder for even longer. Cotton explained to me that the intense heat generated from the lengthy burning process would burn off any oil residue left inside the drum. After the drum had cooled down, the ashes were completely removed, and the inside of the drum was cleaned and brushed with a generous coat of lard (pig fat). A small fire was set to season the inside of the drum, and after this, Cotton's home-made cooking grill was ready for action. Although Cotton's favorite cooking fuel was seasoned oak, for which he would trade seafood, he always used sassafras wood to add smoke flavor to the meat he was grilling. We seldom had beef unless he could arrange a trade with someone who had cows.

One of the things that Cotton liked the most was smoked oysters. During the winter months when the bay waters were cold and the oysters were fat, Daddy liked to get a bed of embers built up after the hardwood had burned down and set unopened oysters in the bed of coals. About an hour before this, he would take some sassafras heartwood pieces and soak them in water. The purpose of this was to slow down the burning process, so that the sassafras would smoke and not flame up. Before he put on the oysters, he would set the sassafras wood on some of the coals until they started to smoke, and then the stage was set. I remember him telling me to be very careful and set each oyster level in the coals so that the liquid would not run out after the shell opened. Within a few minutes, the shells would slowly open about a quarter inch, and the oysters would begin to cook in their own juices. After cooking for about two or three minutes, the oysters were ready to eat. I vividly remember the taste of the smoke from the sassafras wood and the fresh flavor of the open sea from the oysters that brings me back to my childhood.

It is very easy to ascertain that anyone can cook this dish with a minimal amount of experience with grilling. Although Cotton thought that charcoal briquettes were some sort of work of the devil, they will work adequately for this dish; however, I do recommend lump charcoal, since the oysters will absorb flavors quite easily. Sometimes, I feel that the chemical used in processing briquettes impart a taste to the food being grilled, but that may simply be Cotton still talking through me. If you want to be truly authentic, then you will need to gather some hardwood branches or seasoned, cut hardwood, but do not use green hardwood since it will give off a creosote taste to anything you cook. Cut hardwood has to season (or dry out) for about six months to a year before it is ready to cook. Cotton always had some stacks of hardwood that he had traded with a firewood cutter that was seasoning in the shed. Regardless of the type of fuel, you basically need to start sufficient wood, charcoal, etc. afire and let it burn down to embers and you are ready; provided that you have been soaking some pieces of seasoned hardwood in water for about an hour beforehand. Unless you are prepared to make a scavenger hunt out of it, acquiring sassafras wood will be quite a journey. I have managed to always have a pretty good supply on hand since it is so important to me, but I am not willing to tell you my sources. Nestle the unopened oysters in the coals so that they will not lose their liquid during cooking, and you are ready. The oysters cook very quickly and the cooking time will vary depending upon your taste. Some like their oysters less done than others. After experimenting, you will quickly learn how long you prefer to cook yours. After the oysters are done to taste, using heavy leather gloves, hold the bottom shell and cut the top connective tissue from the top shell and remove, leaving the oysters in their bottom shell for serving. Before serving, be sure to cut the bottom connective tissue loose for ease of eating. I suggest that you try an oyster without any sauce to experience the true flavor of the oysters, but you can adorn the oysters with any sauce that you prefer. These make great appetizers and can be beautifully served in a garnished bed of rock salt that has been heated to keep the oysters warm; especially when you follow them up with some crawfish or shrimp éttouffée or stuffed flounder.

Cotton's Smoked Oysters

INGREDIENTS:

12	Unopened medium sized oysters per person
1 bag	Lump charcoal
2 or 3	Chunks of seasoned hardwood
	Your favorite cocktail sauces *(see Dodie's cocktail sauce)*
	Cayenne pepper to taste

About one hour before you plan to begin cooking, place the chunks of seasoned hardwood in a bowl of water that is deep enough to put a weighted object on top of them so they will not float. You can usually find hardwood chunks in the outdoor cooking section of the store. Place sufficient charcoal in your grill to leave a good layer of embers and start the fire, preferably with a charcoal chimney and an electric charcoal lighter, and not starting fluid. Remember that chemical residues will be readily absorbed by the oysters. After the coals are glowing, place the wet hardwood chunks on the edge of the coals so that they are in direct contact with the embers. When they begin to smoke, place your oysters level in the coals and cook for the desired time. I suggest that you begin with two minutes from the time that the oysters first start to open their shells. Raw oyster lovers will probably like less cooking time than others. I like a scant dusting with cayenne, but then, I am a bayou Cajun.

Cotton's Oyster Stew

The only thing that Cotton loved about the colder months of the year was the fact that cold water made oysters taste better. It was during this time that he made his not-so-famous (with anybody but us) oyster stew. I loved eating it with him as a child, mostly because I guess that I loved and admired him so much. Cotton was the strong, silent type, and the ultimate father figure.

His oyster stew had a clean taste that reminded me of the ocean. He was very precise in the ingredients and the way he cooked it. It was a production to behold, and I used to hang over his shoulder and watch intensely. He acted like he hated anybody looking closely while he did anything, but I now think he really did not mind. Cotton was a person of few words, and he seldom verbalized his emotions with anyone, with the possible exception of Cora. You had to learn to interpret when he was really trying to say things like "I'm sorry" or "I enjoy your company" or " I love you," etc. He always seemed to like the fact that I looked forward to eating his oyster stew, and that we liked to eat it together. His version went something like this:

Cotton's Oyster Stew

INGREDIENTS:

1 pint   Oysters
1 stick   Butter (not unsalted)
2 pints   Whole milk
2 tbsps.   Flour
2 tbsps.   Chopped green onions
　　　　 Black pepper to taste

Rinse and drain oysters (do not over-wash), and check for shell particles. In a sauce pan over medium high heat, sauté oysters in butter for one to two minutes or until edges begin to curl.

In a separate container, whisk flour into cold or cool milk until completely mixed. If milk is not cold, the flour will form lumps. Then, pour flour/milk mixture into pan with oysters, and slowly bring to a slight boil, stirring constantly.

After slow boil begins, lower heat and simmer for about two to three minutes to cook flour. Then, turn off heat and stir in green onions and black pepper to taste. Serves four as an appetizer, or two as a soup accompaniment to a seafood entrée.

Cotton and I ate this dish of his at least once a week, often twice a week, during months when the bay water had gotten colder – usually December thru March. Galveston Bay is rather shallow, and the water reacts to colder temperature faster than the deeper ocean water. When the daily temperature reaches the 30's, the bay water cools rather quickly, and the oysters begin to get fatter.

Later in life, when I had married and had my own family, I experimented with Cotton's methods and came up with the following recipe. I shared this with Cotton many times, and was warmed by the fact the Cotton not only liked my version of his stew, but asked that I make it for him many times. I got that same warm feeling of camaraderie when we ate my modified version of his stew.

Cotton's Oyster Stew on Steroids

INGREDIENTS:

1 pint	Oysters
1 stick	Butter (not unsalted)
1 pint	Heavy whipping cream
1 pint	Whole milk
2 tbsp.	Flour
2 tbsp.	Chopped green onions
	Black pepper to taste

Rinse and drain oysters (do not over-wash), and check for shell particles. In a sauce pan over medium high heat, sauté oysters in butter for one to two minutes, or until edges begin to curl. Add in heavy whipping cream and lower heat to medium.

In a separate container, whisk flour into cold or cool milk until completely mixed. If milk is not cold, then flour will form lumps. Then, pour flour/milk mixture into pan with oysters, and slowly bring to a slight boil, stirring constantly.

After slow boil begins, lower heat and simmer for about two to three minutes to cook flour. Then, turn off heat and stir in green onions and black pepper to taste. I have found the salt added to butter to be sufficient, however your taste might desire more salt. Serve with oyster crackers or your favorite cracker. My favorite is "sea toast," which is a large unsalted cracker that is thicker than regular crackers.

Serves four as an appetizer, or two as a soup accompaniment to a seafood entrée.

There are numerous variations, some with cheese, spinach and other associated oyster accompaniments. I am considering sautéing minced jalapenos with oysters in the first step, though I have not tried this yet.

I have made my version of Cotton's oyster stew with lump crab meat and the result was amazing. Substitute crab meat for oysters and shorten the sauté time. *Bon appetite*!

CHAPTER FIFTEEN

COTTON'S PEACH TREE

Cotton's Peach Tree

Cotton did not have many things that he really cherished, except maybe Cora. He was not a man with hobbies or distractions. He lived and breathed his role as the provider without bias. He did, on occasion, take a small amount of pride or pleasure in the acquisition of a certain tool to work with, or maybe a special knife that made his constant net building and repairing easier. He did, however, have a special fondness for peaches, and Cora's homemade peach ice cream. This love led to the acquisition and planting of Cotton's peach tree. Well, actually it was four peach trees that Cotton meticulously planted in the sandy loam of our house on the Bolivar Peninsula. Since the trees were located very close to the area

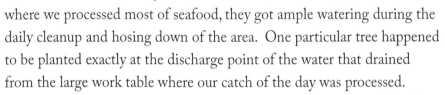

where we processed most of seafood, they got ample watering during the daily cleanup and hosing down of the area. One particular tree happened to be planted exactly at the discharge point of the water that drained from the large work table where our catch of the day was processed.

Since the catch of the day was predominately shrimp which had to have the heads removed by a process known as "heading" (Cajuns were not particularly verbose), and also crabs that had to be cleaned, the discharge water from such processes and the washing down water was very rich in nutrients from the sea. To a peach tree, this was akin to a free buffet at the local hog trough, so this particular peach tree prospered. Although Cotton even said prior to planting the trees that this profusion of what he called "shrimp water" would really make the trees grow, it was evident even he was somewhat surprised at the growth and prosperity of the peach trees, especially that one particular tree that came to be known as Cotton's tree.

As time went on, the trees grew, and Cotton's tree was noticeably larger and more robust. All of the trees did well, but Cotton's tree produced peaches the size of softballs; much bigger than the other trees' fruits. Although Cotton ate many of the peaches from his tree, he relished giving them away to special customers and friends, and especially to my wife Dodie, for whom he had a great fondness. The aroma of the peaches was intoxicating, and seemed to take over our house. Every time I recall this time, I can smell those peaches as if I am still there. I do not think that there are words to describe the airy sweet smell of what seemed to be the perfect peach. I would watch Cotton as he dug small holes around the drip line of his tree, burying pockets of shrimp heads in the ground. Cotton would bring up his special peaches and an old hand cranked ice cream machine, and Cora would make her wonderful peach ice cream.

I'm not sure that many people know today about the process of making ice cream the old fashion way, but it was a rather laborious process. It involved a revolving cylinder with internal counter-rotating paddles that was placed in a large bucket, where it was surrounded by ice that had rock salt sprinkled on it (so that the ice would get colder than its melting point), thereby making the cream mixture in the cylinder freeze as the hand crank is turned, hence ice cream. Seems like a simple process. Well, what they didn't tell you was that as the mixture begins to freeze, the hand crank begins to get even harder to crank. Someone even has to sit on the unit to stabilize it so that the crank can be turned, a job that Cotton always wanted my wife Dodie to do. As a matter of fact, the longer that you are able to turn the crank, the better the consistency of the ice cream becomes, so you are motivated (at least the people not turning the crank are motivated) to turn the crank longer than you really desire. You find yourself wondering if this is really a worth-while venture at all. As you are thinking about turning the couch over to see if there is enough change in it to go buy some ice cream and throw the ice cream maker away, it is finally done.

Possibly due in part to the fact that you are so exhausted from turning the crank, the peach ice cream is heavenly, and you now feel that it was truly worth the effort. There is something indescribable about homemade peach ice cream on one of the Texas gulf coast's 100-plus degree days, when the humidity is so high you feel like you are going to faint, but you are afraid to because you might cook in your own juice.

Cotton's Peach Ice Cream

Even before Cotton had a peach tree, he was very partial to peaches. It was only natural that he would grow peaches at some point in his life. I guess it was Cotton's love of peaches (and also a strong attraction to ice cream) that led Mama to start making homemade peach ice cream. Mama later confided in me that her peach ice cream recipe was simply her vanilla ice cream recipe with peaches added, and a little less vanilla extract. She would start by slightly beating 4 egg yolks, then mixing in 1/8 teaspoons of salt and 2/3 cup of sugar, and finally pouring on about 2 cups of whole milk. When this was completely combined, she would cook this mixture until it was creamy and would "coat da spoon." Cora would then remove the mixture from heat and let it cool. While she was waiting for it to cool, she would peel and mince two large peaches that she had ripened to the soft stage. After mincing, she would mash the peaches with a potato masher, but not completely (so that you could still get very small pieces of peach in the ice cream). She would then add the peaches, 1 and ½ cups of heavy cream and one teaspoon of pure vanilla extract to the mixture. Cora was adamant about using "pure" vanilla extract in anything that called for it, and never imitation vanilla extract. She said that you invest too much time making something like this to not have it turn out perfect.

In the meantime, Cotton was busy getting the old ice cream mixer ready for the task. The crank mechanism would usually have to be oiled so that it would turn freely, since the salt and ice mixture in which it worked made it susceptible to rust. The wooden bucket in which the ice was packed needed to be washed out, and the metal tub and paddle wheel assembly  that actually made the ice cream needed to be washed and sanitized. Once this was completed and Cora had the ice cream mixture ready, she would pour the mixture in the tub and insert the paddle assembly and the cover, and place this in the wooden bucket with the crank mechanism clicked into place. Cotton would go out to the shrimp house and chip off a large piece of the 300-pound bars of ice that we kept on hand for icing shrimp. Cotton was very skilled with an ice pick, having grown up in an era of actually using ice placed in an "ice box," which served as a refrigerator. Securing and inserting a block of ice in the ice compartment of the old ice boxes was a necessary activity. Cotton would begin chipping the ice into small pieces, and layering the ice interspersed with layers of rock salt in the ice bucket that held the metal tub suspended in the center, where the ice cream was made. Once the bucket was topped off with the ice/rock salt layers, a blanket was then placed over the top of the whole thing so that someone could sit on top of the ice cream freezer to hold it steady while everyone else would take turns keeping the crank on the ice cream freezer turning.

Turning the crank handle on the ice cream freezer was no easy task. As the crank was turned, it turned the paddle wheel assembly on the inside of the tub in one direction and the tub in the other direction. The paddle wheel assembly had vertical, wooden blades that scraped the sides of the tub, removing and remixing particles of ice cream as they froze on the inside surface of the tub. Ultimately, the mixture was completely composed of frozen ice cream particles. Well, needless to say, as the mixture was progressing through the freezing cycle, it was becoming progressively more difficult to turn the crank. We would all take turns until we could not turn the crank anymore and then Cotton would always take the final turn. All the while, we would be telling Mama and Daddy that we thought it was ready, and they would be telling us not yet. For some reason, this activity always brought out laughter and camaraderie with us kids wanting to hurry up and eat the ice cream and the folks saying no, not yet. In looking back, the making of ice cream always seemed to bring us together as a family like no other activity did. While one of us would struggle with the crank, the others would playfully tease each other about who was best at turning the crank. All of my memories of the making of ice cream contain laughter and gaiety.

When Cotton took the final turn at the ice cream crank, it was all business. Cotton was a very strong man with large biceps and forearms from many years of lifting heavy loads and pulling on ropes on his shrimp boat. In order to hold the ice cream freezer down while Daddy cranked it, one person would have to sit on the lap of another. We were constantly falling off and having to have the others hold us steady so that Cotton could turn the crank. And then, as if some moment had come to Cotton in a flush of inspiration, he would calmly say, "it's ready." You are then supposed to repack the freezer bucket with more ice and more rock salt, and wait for about 30 minutes or so to allow the ice cream to completely freeze. In a room full of children who are dripping with anticipation, not to mention the temperature outside likely being in the triple digits, the thought of waiting another 30 minutes was too much to bear. As if all simultaneously inspired, we would run to Mama, knowing full well that she was a pushover where children were concerned. To my recollection, we never waited the extra 30 minutes for the ice cream to freeze. Mama always let us eat it immediately, frequently not getting any for herself – telling us that she did not want any, but that was just Mama.

The days of the manual crank ice cream freezer are probably forever gone, but there are plenty of electric ice cream freezers available for making homemade ice cream today. If you would like to try your hand at making some of Cora's ice cream, then I have her recipe for you.

Cotton's (Cora's) Peach Ice Cream

INGREDIENTS:

4	Egg yolks (slightly beaten)
⅛ tsp.	Salt
⅔ cup	Sugar
2 cups	Whole milk
1 ½ cups	Heavy cream
1 tsp.	Pure vanilla extract
2	Large peaches, ripened to the soft stage, peeled and sectioned

After mixing the egg yolks, salt and sugar in a bowl, add in the milk and cook in a double boiler until the mixture becomes very creamy; able to coat a large stirring spoon. In a food processor, blend the peaches until there are only some very small pieces still remaining, then blend into the cooled mixture, along with the heavy cream and vanilla. At this point, you freeze according to the instructions for your particular ice cream freezer.

Cora also made a very good vanilla ice cream by taking the above recipe, increasing the pure vanilla to 2 teaspoons, and eliminating the peaches. I'm sure that she would have encouraged you to scrape the inside of a vanilla bean into the mixture if she would have had access to vanilla beans in her time.

Cora's Old Time Cobbler

Mama cooked an old style fruit cobbler that was made free standing on a cookie sheet, and not in a pan. Mama said that when she was young, they did not have much cookware, and there was not always a cooking vessel for every purpose. She said that her Mama used to cook wild berry pies this way, and that she had adapted it to peaches for "ya Daddy." In addition to tasting good, this dish makes an impressive presentation. I have prepared this for my friends and family on many occasions, and it always leaves an impression. Feel free to adapt this to your favorite fruit or berry.

INGREDIENTS:

Crust:
- 2 cups All purpose flour (preferably unbleached)
- 1 ½ Sticks cold butter
- ½ tsp. Salt
- 4-8 tbsps. Cold water

Filling:
- 4 cups Prepared and cut-up fruits i.e. peaches, nectarines, blackberries, dew berries, apples, etc.
- ½-¾ c. Sugar (to your desired sweetness)
- ⅓ cup Corn starch

As with any pie crust, work with cold ingredients to try and not melt the butter prior to baking for flaky crust. Combine the salt and flour, and then (using a pie crust tool), cut in the butter until the mixture resembles corn or cracker meal. At this stage, the dough should form a ball and hold its shape. Without handling too much, form the dough into a thick patty on waxed paper and refrigerate for ½ to one hour.

Roll out dough on a lightly-floured surface to form a circle that is about twice as thick as regular pie dough, and place on a large cookie sheet. Combine the sugar and corn starch, and thoroughly coat the fruit. Place the coated fruit mixture in the center of the crust, and fold the edges up and over the fruit mixture, leaving an opening in the center for steam to escape during baking. Crimp the folds of the crust around the top of the cobbler and pinch so that they will hold their shape. Brush top of cobbler with egg wash and sprinkle with sugar.

Bake at 350 for 45 minutes to one hour, or until browned to your preference.

Cotton's Love of Coffee

Cotton loved coffee. He would begin and end his day with coffee, as well as filling in most of the spaces in between. Even though he would occasionally appreciate *café au lait* (pronounced *caffay o lay,* meaning coffee with milk or hot milk) and sometimes French coffee mixed with chickory, Cotton preferred *café noir* (pronounced *caffay nor,* meaning black coffee, or coffee without anything added) that was made with medium to dark roasted coffee beans, and brewed by the pour-over brewing method. Pour-over brewing is accomplished in a coffee pot, often called a drip pot, where hot water is poured into a vessel that is mounted atop a strainer into which ground coffee is placed. The water slowly drains or "drips" through the ground coffee into a holding vessel that is mounted directly under the strainer. The Cajun French word for coffee pot is *grégue* (pronounced *grr reg'*).

In his early years, Cotton roasted small quantities of green coffee beans until they were to his liking, and ground them in a hand grinder which was mounted on the kitchen wall (as was customary in Cajun homes in the early 1900's). As time journeyed on, civilization came to the bayous, and Cotton was able to get his favorite coffee, which could only be gotten at an early food store that has since faded into obscurity. The store brand of coffee came in whole bean form that could be ground right in the store with a large mechanical grinder. This was as close to "Star Wars" technology that a bayou Cajun could get. Cotton would take a one pound bag of medium roast beans and a one pound bag of dark roast beans, and pour both bags into the grinder at the same time. He would then turn on the grinder and fill both bags with the resultant medium/dark

"Pour-over" coffee pot

roast grinds. He would usually double or triple up this process when we were at that particular store, since the only time he could get his favorite brand of coffee was when we "went to town."

Cotton's day began very early, usually between 2:00 and 4:00 am, depending upon which particular seafood was in season. He was always the first person to rise in the house, and he would immediately go about the process of making coffee. Even though he made every effort to be quiet, there was always a crescendo of pot and pans crashing out onto the floor as Cotton tried to assemble the coffee pot parts. All the while, Cotton was issuing forth expletives in modified whisper form, as he attempted, always unsuccessfully, to catch the cascading cookware. There was never a need for an alarm clock in our house. When Cotton was up, we were all up. It never seemed to make me angry to awaken in this manner. Now, as I look back on those mornings, I get a rather warm, "that's my dad" sort of feeling.

I would usually not immediately arise to all of this organized confusion. I preferred to wait until I sensed that glorious smell of fresh-brewed coffee. I remember the warm glow of anticipation that came with the fresh coffee smell that filled the house, a smell that warms me as I write this as if it were occurring this minute. The only thing that would awaken a body that was wracked with the activities associated with post-pubescent pursuits was a cup or two of Cotton's finest. Cotton also brought a large thermos bottle filled with coffee to make it through the day on the boat. What do you give a man that has everything?

Even though Cotton drank his coffee plain without the need for any of the customary additives, there were occasions where he liked to "mix it up a bit" with something special. One of his special brews was to make what he called pecan coffee. This was also a favorite of mine and I still make it occasionally when I want to think about Cotton.

Cotton's Pecan Coffee

INGREDIENTS:

8 tsps. Good medium ground coffee
1 cup Pecans (mashed)
Hot water sufficient to make 8 to 10 cups of coffee

In the strainer basket of a drip pot, add the coffee and top it with the mashed pecans. Assemble the coffee pot, and slowly pour the hot water over the coffee strainer. Cotton and I both liked this coffee plain or black; however, it can be served with cream, whipped cream and sugar if you prefer.

Unfortunately for many of you, this can only be successfully made in a pour-over drip pot. The reason for this is the fact that the mashed pecans will slow the flow of the water through the coffee, making a percolator-type coffee maker and a normal coffee maker over-flow. With a pour-over drip coffee maker, you can slowly add the hot water to keep it from over-flowing. If you like the flavor of coffee as much as I do and you are able to brew this coffee, I assure you it will be worth the effort for an occasional change of pace.

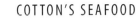

CHAPTER SIXTEEN

LIFE, LOVE, & THE PURSUIT OF CRAWFISH

Life, Love and the Pursuit of Crawfish

Crawfish, crawdad, mudbug, Cajun lobster, and a host of other names (some not so flattering) is a small, freshwater crustacean found basically throughout the world but in particularly large quantities in southern Louisiana. It seems that the swamps and marshes of Southwestern Louisiana and the eastern tip of Texas are ideal places for crawfish to proliferate. That is, until the Cajuns came along.

The fact that Cajuns eat *ecrevisse* (pronounced *ah cra veese'*, meaning crawfish) and have always done so is a pretty well-established fact. Now, it seems that everyone everywhere is eating crawfish, and talking as if they have always eaten crawfish, and paying exorbitant sums to eat crawfish. For a minute, let's put this into historical context. Before the Cajun culture became a point of interest and during the time when Cajuns were talked about with some

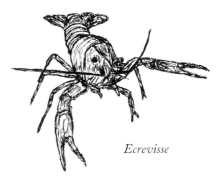

Ecrevisse

degree of trepidation, crawfish were considered water insects which grew in some foul ditch somewhere. Now it seems that those same people who were repulsed at the thought of crawfish, much less at the thought of putting one in their mouth, are having crawfish boils and eating them in vast quantities. In the midst of the festivities, however, a Cajun would remind them that they forgot to suck on the heads.

As a bayou Cajun who ultimately left the marshes for a college education and other pursuits, I have to admit that sucking on a crawfish head does not appear to be something that you would have learned from Amy Vanderbilt. Actually, sucking on the heads is not a requirement to eat and enjoy boiled crawfish, but it has somehow become a weird point of pride for Cajuns, and also a way to send chills down the spine of the social elite. For Cajuns, a crawfish boil has a social aspect that is mostly misunderstood by non-Cajuns.

When you settle down to a platter of boiled crawfish, the idea of getting full means that you are going to be there for a while (since the meat to shell ratio on crawfish is rather low). It is during this time, that you talk about life, love, anguish and anxiety – all the favorite topics of Cajuns. As a child, I remember sitting for hours peeling crawfish and listening to the old folks talk about adventures in the marsh. Close brushes with death and other tales of growing up in the swamps were my favorites. There were no televisions at this point in history, and few Cajuns even had radios (although we did). A crawfish boil was a time that you could sit down with each other and just talk because you were going to be there for a while. Only after a considerable amount of conversation (and beer drinking) has occurred do people really start to reveal their true selves. It's some sort of indefinable threshold where people run out of superficial conversation, and their thoughts and fears leak out in dribs and drabs. Eventually, the pieces start to collect, and you begin to discover that all people live, love, laugh and cry; just about different things. Cajuns are somehow aware that it is this commonality that binds us together and makes us closer; without it, we languish as a people and a culture.

As a young child in the early 1950's, we lived on the outskirts of the small commercial fishing village of Sabine Pass, Texas. There was a very large ditch across the street from our house that was the main drain for a large marsh area surrounding Pole Lake and Texas Bayou. I became adapt at a cast net at a very young age, and was able to catch enough crawfish to boil when fresh water was draining out of the marsh. To bait the crawfish to my spot, I would go to the shrimp boat docks with my dad and catch a half dozen or so blue crabs. After crushing them thoroughly to expose the inner flesh, I would throw them in the ditch where I intended to cast my net. Every hour or so would yield a net full of large crawfish, and soon we had enough to boil. After we ate what we wanted, Mama would send me to give some to the neighbors, because Mama believed in sharing. Oddly enough, I often was met with negativity. It seems that people characteristically grow tired of something that they can have often and free.

Now, it seems that everybody everywhere wants to eat boiled crawfish. As demand goes higher, it is only basic economics that the prices will definitely follow. Currently, live crawfish for boiling are selling in excess of $2.50* per pound, and these prices are in areas of close proximity to where they are grown. Because of their high shell to meat ratio, this would put the actual cost of the meat at around $12.00 to $15.00 per pound. If you were to factor in cost for areas of the country more remotely located from the source, the prices would be much higher. It appears that a commodity that was for the most part free for the taking for the average Bayou Cajun has now priced those very folks out of the market.

This is a spring, 2015 price is for mixed (sizes) sold in approximately 30 lb. sacks in Jefferson County, Texas in the eastern most section of the state where crawfish are grown.

Cora's Boiled Crawfish

Cajuns are not the only people who have ever eaten crawfish; however, Cajuns have certainly elevated the eating of crawfish to an art form (a term used rather loosely in reference to Cajuns). A Cajun crawfish boil was usually more of a social gathering than it was a meal. As mentioned, crawfish have a very little meat relative to their size – something on the order of maybe 85% shell and 15%

meat (my estimate). The head of the crawfish is disproportionately large in relation to the body when compared to some of its crustacean cousins like shrimp or lobster. Because of the relatively small tail of the crawfish (which houses the meat one eats), the eating of crawfish involves going through many crawfish in an attempt to satisfy even the most basic of hunger. Hence, the social gathering aspect of crawfish eating.

Sitting at long, home-made tables covered in something we called "oil-cloth" – you know, the ones that were red and white checkered and were used in old road-side diners – I can still hear Mama telling us stories about her childhood while we all sat peeling and eating crawfish. The crawfish were steaming hot right after they came from the large, three-legged cast iron pot Mama used to boil crawfish in over a wood burning fire. I can still remember the smell of the burning salt cedar wood that Daddy gathered from the ridge. Not much else besides salt cedars grew there, except maybe a few live oaks on some of the higher ground. Even when there was some other wood in the fire, the salt cedars aroma still seemed to dominate the air.

Mama would start the fire an hour or two before the gathering to get a large bed of coals built up. Before she started the fire, she would arrange three large flat stones so that the cast iron pot would rest right above the coals. Once a good bed of coals had formed, she and Daddy would place the boiling pot on the three stones that the legs rested on and fill the pot a little over half full of water. As the water was heating up, Mama would add her boiling seasonings to the pot along with onions, lemons, and sometimes other vegetables such as corn on the cob, celery, garlic, whatever pepper she had growing at the time and occasionally smoked sausage.

Another chore while waiting for the water to boil was purging the crawfish. Since crawfish eat, go to work and live in the mud, they have a tendency to be rather dirty when caught, with a lot of swamp borne particles in and about their shells. Crawfish breathe by taking in water through their gills and extracting the oxygen from the water, which is also muddy. It is therefore not enough to simply rinse them off with running water to clean them. Mama was especially keen on getting the crawfish as mud-free as possible, so she had a purge method that I use to this day. Mama would put the crawfish in a no. 3 (large) tub and fill it with clean water. She would then let the crawfish "breathe" in the clean water for about 15 minutes, and all the while they were breathing out the mud. She would then pour off the water in the tub and refill it with more clean water to repeat the step. Only after two fresh water purges would she use the standard way to purge crawfish, and that was to add salt to the purge water and leave the crawfish for about another 15 minutes. Mama said that the salt water purge would start to kill the crawfish, and she did not want to boil any crawfish that were not alive when placed in the boiling water.

By now, the water was boiling and the smell of Mama's seafood boiling seasonings had filled the air. Her boiling pot would hold about 60 to 70 pounds of crawfish, which boiled for about 10 minutes, give or take. Immediately after adding the crawfish, she would pour 4 to 6 bottles of beer into the pot and give it a good stir.

Mama would start taking out and trying a crawfish or two until she was satisfied that they were cooked properly; then, she would remove the crawfish using a large, long handled wire basket that Daddy had made for Mama to use for boiling seafood. She would then add another round of seasonings and crawfish (depending upon the number of people to be fed). The steaming hot crawfish were placed on large metal trays, which were then placed at several spots along the long tables, usually arranged end to end. To each tray of crawfish, Mama would pour about a cup or two of good whiskey and give the hot crawfish a good stir. I remember Mama always had a bottle of bourbon around when we boiled crawfish.

The grown folks drank beer (or sometimes wine that someone had made) with their boiled crawfish, and the children drank home-made root beer that Mama always had. Excitement filled the air as cousins, aunts, uncles and friends all sat down to a true delight. As everyone settled in to the peeling and eating ritual of a crawfish boil (and the day to day occurrences had been lightly discussed), the conversation turned to parties and get-togethers of the past, and exploits of days gone by, which was my favorite part of a seafood boil. Mama told some of the most interesting and thought-provoking stories which usually involved exploits of her father, mother and grandparents. Daddy told of times and incidents of his life, usually while hunting or catching seafood. I can still see the look on Mama's face as she told stories in great detail that made you feel as if you were watching from a branch overhead as the story unfolded. There was always a small mystery in Mama's stories that was not completely revealed – an edge that you were brought to but that you could not completely see over. Daddy's stories were more straight to the point, but not predictable, so there was still very much interest on our part. Daddy usually told of strange but true situations he became involved in while on his boat catching seafood or while running his traps.

Well, fast forward to today. Over the years, I have continued to boil crawfish in Mama's tradition; however, I have modernized somewhat with the addition of liquid crab boil mix. The following recipe works quite well for today's tastes, but remains essentially true to Mama's original recipe for boiled crawfish.

Boiled Crawfish

INGREDIENTS:

12 qts. Water
3 boxes Dry crab boil mix (3 oz.)
8 oz. Bottle of liquid crab boil
1 tbsp. Olive oil
¼-⅓ cup Salt (to taste, but should be somewhat salty)
2-4 Bottles of beer
2 Lemons (whole)
4 Stems of celery (washed and halved)
4 Ears of corn (shucked and halved – can use frozen half ears)
3-4 lbs. Small red potatoes (skins on/washed and brushed)
10 lbs. Crawfish
Optional:
2 Dried cayenne pepper (split longways)
1 cup Whiskey (bourbon or blended, your choice)

In a large stock pot (16 qt. or larger), combine the water, liquid crab boil, salt, one dried cayenne pepper (if using) and one box of dry crab boil (with the mesh bag torn open), and bring to a boil. Add red potatoes and boil until potatoes are fork tender. When potatoes are done, remove from boiling water and place in a bowl covered with a towel to keep them warm.

To the boiling water, add the other two boxes of dry crab boil mix, and re-salt a little if desired since the potatoes will absorb some of the salt. Add crawfish, corn, celery, and beer. Cut lemons in half, squeeze juice in boiling water and drop halves in the water. Return mixture to boil and continue boiling for 8 to 10 minutes, depending upon the size of the crawfish. Remember, you can remove and peel a crawfish at different points during boiling to test for desired doneness. Remove crawfish from boiling water and serve hot with Dodie's red sauce (recipe follows). Serve the potatoes and corn with butter, along with celery. When served as an appetizer, allow 3 to 4 lbs. of crawfish per person. When served as a main course, allow about 5 to 7 pounds per person (or 10 to 15 pounds per Cajun).

If you opt to use the whiskey like Mama did, then you are in for a treat. Immediately after removing the crawfish from the boiling water, pour the whiskey over the steaming crawfish and stir them to coat. Mama's crawfish were always the best.

When you are eating the boiled crawfish, every good Cajun knows that you need a good red sauce, and my wife makes the best red sauce I have ever tasted. I detailed it earlier in the book, but I am going to include it again so that you will not have to go looking for it.

Dodie's Red Sauce

INGREDIENTS:

12 oz. Ketchup (about ½ a bottle)
1-2 tbsps. Prepared horseradish (or 3 or 4)
1 tbsp. Lime juice (to taste)

Again, she does not really measure these ingredients but instead makes adjustments to taste, and it always comes out. We like it very hot, so she leans more toward using a lot of horseradish. After you make this a couple of times, you will quickly learn your preferences.

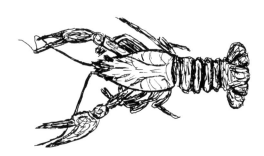

Cora's Crawfish Étouffée

Crawfish *étouffée* (pronounced *et too faye'*) was one of my favorite crawfish dishes. Étoufée is a rich, Cajun stew that can be made with shrimp as well as crawfish, but there is something special about the crawfish version. We always had an abundance of crawfish available during their season in the late spring, and I was always ready for Mama's crawfish étouffée. I remember sitting with Mama after a crawfish boil, helping her peel the leftover crawfish and anticipating an étouffée. Conversations with Mama, especially during monotonous chores like peeling crawfish, usually were about her early childhood and her cooking expeditions. I guess that is why I cook so much to this day, because Mama made cooking sound so adventurous.

This dish can be made with regular roux; however, the use of a butter roux is recommended (see "Roux, Cajun Style"). As I sit in front of my computer, I can smell the roux cooking as if I were still there in Mama's little kitchen.

Cora's Crawfish Étouffée

INGREDIENTS:

For the butter roux:
   2 sticks   Butter (salted)
   1 cup   Flour
   2   Large yellow onions (one chopped and one sliced to make thin rings)
Additional ingredients:
   1 cup   Chopped celery
   1   Large chopped green bell pepper
   6 cups   Water (can be chicken stock or seafood stock if desired)
   6 cups   Crawfish meat – raw or cooked
   1 cup   Chopped green onions

½ cup   Chopped fresh parsley
1 clove   Minced garlic
1 tsp.   Black pepper or to taste
½ tsp.   Cayenne pepper or to taste
1 tsp.   Salt or to taste
          Filé (if desired) to taste

In a large cast iron dutch oven, make a butter roux with the butter and flour, stirring constantly until medium-to-dark brown, and then stir in onions, bell pepper and celery, and cook for about 3 to 5 minutes. Stir water or stock into the roux/vegetable mixture until thoroughly blended, then add in salt, pepper and garlic, and simmer for about 30 minutes uncovered. Stir in crawfish meat and cook for about 20 to 30 minutes (if raw) or about 10 minutes (if using cooked crawfish). Add in onion rings and simmer for about 10 minutes until rings are softened. Turn off heat and stir in parsley and green onions. Serve or rice that has been dusted with filé along with French bread.

Shrimp étouffée can be made with the above recipe by substituting shrimp for the crawfish. I like the shrimp version which I frequently had growing because the crawfish season was rather short when compared to that of the shrimping season. We were in the shrimp business and we always had shrimp. Because of their fat content, there is a certain richness that only crawfish can bring to this dish so I have to say that crawfish etouffee' is probably my favorite crawfish dish.

Currently, crawfish have become available at almost all times of the year cleaned and frozen. Many of these are imported crawfish that have a very strong taste that I have sometimes found to be rather unpleasant. When you seek out cleaned and frozen crawfish to make this and other dishes, I would encourage you to try to get crawfish that are caught and processed in Louisiana or Texas. I have had better luck using more locally processed crawfish in all of my dishes.

CHAPTER SEVENTEEN

KEITH LAKE

Keith Lake

The setting for a good portion of my childhood adventures was a body of water known as Keith Lake. In actuality, Keith Lake was not a lake at all, but merely the final intersection with civilization of a series of shallow, marshy, oval-shaped lakes that were interconnected from the deep marsh to the intersection of highway 87 at Keith Lake. There were actually two intersections, one that was a natural cut to the mouth of the Sabine River (which was salt water at this point), and the other was at the small piece of property that my Uncle George and Aunt Rita owned, upon which they lived and ran a small seafood shop. The remainder of the property surrounding Keith Lake was owned by a land and cattle family whose wealth emerged during the Spindletop oil boom of East Texas around the 1900's. There were several conditions under which my Uncle was allowed to own the land and operate a seafood business. Uncle George had to have and maintain a boat launch (for which, he could charge a user fee), and also regulate who used the launch. At the time, the only authorized users of the launch were a local hunting and fishing club that had a lease with the wealthy family. The other condition (which was not frequently used) was that my Uncle George had to guide the family members of the land owners and their guests on duck hunts during the hunting seasons.

It was the uniqueness of the geological occurrence of Keith Lake and its interconnected sister lakes – Big Shell Lake, Little Shell Lake, Big Clam Lake, Little Clam Lake, Star Lake, Knight's Lake, etc. – that made all of this so wondrous. The majority of my experiences occurred in what we called Big Shell Lake, which was the first interconnected lake to Keith Lake (also known as Johnson Lake), and with the next interconnected lake that we called Little Shell Lake (which was also known as Shell Lake). Cajuns often times name things and places

Jim holding a black drum caught on Keith Lake, circa 1951

for themselves, which could be a throwback to the self-imposed isolationism after *Le Grand De'rangement* (the Great Upheaval). The remainder of the lakes were connected by a rather lengthy waterway known as Salt Bayou, which we called the Ten Mile Cut. The tributaries to Ten Mile Cut connected Big Mud Lake (also known as Salt Lake), Little Mud Lake (also known as Fence Lake) and also Knight Lake, which for some reason we did not rename. The Ten Mile Cut ran thru Little Clam Lake and Big Clam Lake (popularly known as simply Clam Lake), finally terminating at Star Lake.

The large marshy expanse surrounding all of the interconnected lakes of the Keith Lake complex became my entire world, or perhaps more accurately the world that I grew to prefer. The natural tidal cut to a salt water source (coupled with the fresh water drainage of the inland marsh) created a perfect estuary for the birthing and incubation of numerous forms of aquatic creatures. As I enter the twilight period of my life, I remember my youth as a time of freedom and discovery. Any anguish or apprehension of the dangers and strife of life back during that time of my life have seemed to fade. It's rather curious to me now how, as a youth, I thought that I would never leave my life on the salt marshes; then after college, I hooked up to the plow harness of civilization. I awoke daily, and pulled that plow of responsibility and duty to build a life that modern man has decided is good and desirable. Now, it seems that I actually had it right the first time, but these are the musings of an aging man. I spent my formative years on Keith Lake, from my earliest remembrances until about the age of 17.

I was born in 1946, near the end of World War II. At the time, my dad Cotton was working on one of the larger shrimping vessels (or "offshore boats" as they were called). This left me, mom and my three older sisters home alone for four- to five-day periods, which was the usual time period that the offshore boats were away from port.

Coincidental to our situation was the fact that my Uncle George and Aunt Rita liked to travel, and they arranged for me, my mom and sisters to stay with their five children, and run the house and seafood business on Keith Lake. I know to some people, this would sound like a nightmare; however, to my mom Cora, this was heaven. She loved children and they loved her. Cora had a way of talking, and subsequently being, on the same level with children. My mom always made you feel that what you were talking about was important, and she also had a way to make the everyday work of running the family business adventurous, and even fun. She would organize work details, and invent competitions that made the large amount of work involved with running the business somewhat entertaining. She also organized work details around large family meals, the main dishes of which were chosen at different times by everyone in the group. Every day seemed like more fun that actual work.

Since this all began when I was about two or three years old, almost all of my earliest childhood recollections seem to fade in at Keith Lake. Of the nine children in the group, I was the youngest, and one of my cousins at about twenty years was the oldest. The closest person to me by age in the group was my cousin Ernest Ray (nicknamed "Coony"), who was about ten years older than I was. It was Coony who I always worked with as a "header" (removing heads from the shrimp sold for eating), and as a "culler" (removing unwanted catch from the shrimp) on the small shrimp boat that he ran. Additionally, I was the light man and spotter when we hunted alligators at night. Except for work times, I was left to my own devices. There were no neighborhood children to play with since the nearest house was about five miles away in the small seaport town of Sabine Pass, Texas.

Ernest Ray (Coony) LaBove, Joyce LaBove, and John Alladin (JA) LaBove, circa 1937

A typical work day for Coony and I would begin at about 2 in the morning, since we were catching live shrimp to sell to the fishermen heading for the coast at just before sunrise. The night before, we would load a sack or two of fish meal on the boat that we traded for with workers at the local menhaden plant down the road from our house. Once at the trawling area that we designated by driving two large poles into the lake about 200 feet apart, we would wet the fish meal and form it into large balls that we would then slowly ease into the water, so that they would sink to the bottom and not float off. This was done in the shape of a large oval that corresponded with the path of our net during trawling. By the next morning, the shrimp had moved in to feast on the fish meal, and would be waiting on us. We would drop the nets and pull them for approximately five minutes, or one oval pass called a "drag," so that the shrimp would not be drowned in the net (since we were selling these as live bait). They were dropped into a live bait tank that was on the boat. After about 2 drags around the oval, we would run back to the bait house (about ½ mile) to transfer the live shrimp to the holding tanks for sale to the fishermen, who were due to arrive shortly. We would repeat this scenario once more, and we usually then had sufficient live bait for our customers.

By sun rise, we had customarily sold out of live shrimp, and it was time to head back to the baited area and make more drags for what we called "eatin' shrimp," or those that were not sold for bait but for consumption. Coony and I would now drag the nets for about fifteen to twenty minute time periods (since keeping these shrimp alive was not a consideration), making wider concentric circles with each pass. After a couple of drags, we would have caught most of the shrimp that were there, and we would return to the bait house to ice them down for sale to customers looking for shrimp to eat.

My other cousins had other duties, including running crab traps for crabs to sell, running muskrat traps, skinning and stretching the muskrat hides for sale to the hide buyer who occasionally came around, and whatever seasonal seafood occurrence that we found ourselves in at the time. Usually several times a week, Cora would gather all of us together, and we would decide on an activity that was always accompanied by food. A favorite of everybody in the crowd was Cora's stuffed crabs, which seemed to be picked by informal vote (or lobbying) of the group every other time. Once decided, Cora would assign two-person groups to different tasks. She would assign some to boil the crabs, then some to clean them, then we would all sit down and pick out crab meat. All the while, Cora was keeping everybody entertained with stories of her youth and family lore. Some would be assigned the task of cleaning and brushing the backs of the crabs for stuffing, and others would be doing the stuffing. Then Cora would fry them, and we would all sit down to eat

These were my musical cousins in 1985, playing at a cajun party.
From left, standing: Coony LaBove, harmonica; Woodrow Tyler, sticks;
Joyce LaBove, harmonica. From left, sitting: Raymond LaBove, guitar;
George LaBove, accordian; JA LaBove, spoons.

with conversation and much laughter mandatory. After we all ate, Cora would break out the ice cream freezer and we would take turns cranking it and sitting on it to keep it steady, and then we would eat ice cream and play Cajun music on whatever instruments we had. The harmonica and accordion always carried the body of the music, and impromptu items like washboards and spoons were used as percussion instruments. Everybody could join in with something. We even had a "tub bass" that one of my cousins made. A tub bass is a no. 3 metal washtub that is placed face-down on the floor, with an eye bolt in the center attached to a broom stick with a wire. When the broom stick is placed on the rim of the tub and the wire is stretched tight and plucked, the tone can be varied by changing the tension on the wire by pulling back on the broom stick. Voila – you get a pretty respectable bass fiddle. At some point in life, you come to the conclusion that

223

happiness is only driven by expectations. If you awaken with no expectations of the day, happiness is just a chance encounter away. We were a group of people placed in circumstances that were enriched by Cora, and though we had very few material things (even for the times), I struggle even now to remember ever feeling anything but exuberance for those times and experiences.

Alligator Sauce Piquant

Our family grew up around alligators, and they were a part of our daily lives. Cajuns interacted with numerous animals in the marsh, but none were quite like the alligator. Alligators have existed for millions of years and have changed very little  during that period, which is usually a sign that nature got it right the first time. This might be all well and good for the alligator, but it does not bode well for Cajuns. Like many creatures that are at the top of their particular food chain, alligators seem to exist to cull out the old, weak and infirm animals, but sometimes in the process, they also manage to kill and eat some young and healthy animals (along with an occasional Cajun). It did not take very long for Cajuns to decide that they did not want any part of the alligator food chain thing. Daily observation of the ways that alligators work and play very quickly teaches you how to deal with (and coexist with) them.

Alligators are not mean-spirited creatures that spend their days trying to kill and eat people. In fact, nature did not seem to design the entirety of the who-eats-who schedule with human beings in mind. This actually is not true, since at one time many millions of years ago, man was definitely a food source for numerous creatures, both land and sea. It seems that, for whatever reason – the opposing thumb, the ability to walk upright, discovery of fire or simply the desire not to be eaten – mankind took himself out of the mix, and in doing so actually became the top predator in everybody's food chain. It seems that human beings will eat anything. This does not mean that we could not be killed and eaten by any of the other animals; it simply means that we have the ability to avoid being eaten if we pay attention. After watching the way that an alligator catches and kills it prey, and how aggressively it protects its nesting places, Cajuns very quickly decided that they did not want any part of that. Every (live) Cajun knows not to enter the water where alligators live and work. They also know not to approach an alligator nest during mating season, and to never, ever feed alligators. With some exceptions, alligators (like almost all other animals) would prefer to avoid humans. Over time, it seems that all animals have discovered that mankind is dangerous and cannot be trusted. When cornered or placed in a position to protect its young, any animal will fight back. In the case of alligators, fighting back can have fatal results.

The marsh is a wondrous place filled with sights, sounds and sensations found nowhere else. The marshes where I grew up had a salt sea smell that made me feel comfortable and at home. The alligators were there, along with other dangerous creatures, but observations soon tell you what to do and not to do. City dwellers would probably think that you are so occupied with thoughts of self-preservation that you could not think of or do anything else in such an environment, but nothing is further from the truth. In fact, I scarcely thought about any of the dangers when I was working and playing in the marsh. It was as though there was a part of my brain that subconsciously dealt with these dangers and guided me around them, so that I could perceive and enjoy the beauty around me. I am quite sure that there would be those who would say that it was irresponsible of the adults in my life to have allowed me the freedom to engage with the elements of the marshes at such a young age, but we were raised to understand the dangers and perils of such an engagement. Although I knew and understood the dangers, at no time do I ever remember being afraid to go out into the marshes, whether it was for work or play. Moreover, I actually felt at home in the marsh, with the smell of the salty air and the sound of the winds rustling through the salt grass and bull rushes. However, there were times in the marsh when a little serious thought was required, and one most definitely was when you went to hunt and kill alligators.

Somewhere early in Cajun history, it was discovered that certain people would pay pretty well for the hides of alligators. Since Cajuns were already trapping other animals for their hides, alligators were a rather natural inclusion. The only problem was that alligators did not like to give up their skins, and they fought back; sometimes, they fought back violently. Over time, Cajuns learned to deal with the tenacity of the alligator, and they became adapt at the taking of alligators for hide and for food. My family had been hunting alligators for their hides for

Photo courtesy of Joyce LaBove

many years before I came along, and for me, the taking of alligators was all quite natural. We sold the hides, ate the meat of the tail (and the legs if it was a large alligator), and used the remaining parts for bait in our traps. Although truthfully I have to say that alligator was not among my favorite dishes, there were some notable exceptions, and one of those was alligator sauce *piquant* (pronounced *pe con'*).

Aunt Rita in the mid-1940's

My Aunt Rita made this dish, and it was always something that I liked. Although I am not usually fond of tomato-based dishes, I always liked this one. Aunt Rita would begin by marinating overnight the pieces of cut-up alligator meat in a mixture of red wine vinegar, chopped yellow onions, chopped green onions, olive oil, peppercorns, bay leaves and a splash of dry red wine. The sauce piquant would start with three large cans of tomatoes, one cup each of minced yellow onions, bell peppers, and celery, about a half cup of red wine vinegar and a splash of dry red wine. She would then simmer the sauce for about an hour, adjusting the liquid with tomato juice when necessary. While the sauce was simmering, she would salt, pepper and flour the pieces of alligator, deep-fry them until golden brown, and set them aside. After the sauce was ready, she would place the fried alligator in the sauce and simmer for about another half hour. She would then serve over rice. Aunt Rita was a very good cook, and this was only one of many dishes that she cooked for me over the years.

Cora's Red Fish Courtbouillon

Cora referred to this dish as fish *courtbouillon* (pronounced *coo be yawh'*), and her recipe was one of the best I have ever tasted. I always liked Mama's version for several reasons; the most notable of which was her use of a butter roux base. Mama had several dishes with which she preferred the use of a butter-based roux, and this was one of them (see "butter roux" in section on making roux). Mama also never used the head of the red fish in making her courtbouillon, as was customary with many Cajun versions of this dish. It was Cora's contention that the head and bones of a red fish were too oily and strong-tasting for any dish. She even cut away any "red meat" along the centerline of the fillets of the red fish before she used them in any recipe.

We always had an abundance of red fish, or "channel bass" as they were commonly referred. Not only were red fish caught in the shrimp trawl, but Cotton waded the front marsh and cast netted them in tidal pools for market. At low tides, the tidal pools would trap red fish in the shallows where they had been feeding, and here Cotton would cast his large cast net. He would net very large red fish; quite often running over thirty pounds each, which he sold for extra money. These large red fish would yield very large, thick fillets which made the best courtbouillon.

Cora would take the fillets and cut them into very large cubes, about two to three inches on a side, for her courtbouillon. Although you can use just about any fish for courtbouillon, Mama said that red fish held together better because of its coarse flesh with very large flakes, making it the best fish for this purpose. If you want to prepare this dish, you are going to have to either catch your own red fish or find one that has been farm-raised to purchase. The commercial sale of wild-caught red fish is currently prohibited in most, if not all, states due to over-fishing.

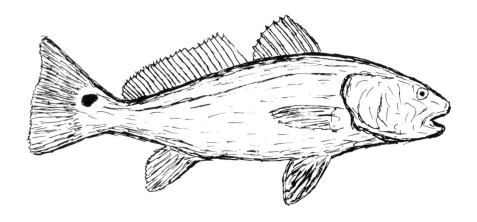

Cora's Red Fish Courtbouillon

INGREDIENTS:

5 lbs.	Red fish cut into pieces, preferably thick cubes
5 tbsp.	Flour
5 tbsp.	Melted butter
3	Large yellow onions
4 ribs	Celery
1	Large bell pepper
2 cloves	Minced garlic
2 ½ qts.	Water or stock (Mama sometimes used chicken stock)
2 cans	Diced tomatoes
1 can	Diced tomatoes with chills
1	Large can tomato paste
1-1½ cup	Chopped green onion tops

In a deep iron pot, make a roux with the melted butter and flour. When roux is the proper shade of brown, add in onions and stir until onions start to brown, then add in celery bell pepper and minced garlic. Cook for another minute or two then gradually incorporate water or stock until all is thoroughly blended, adding in all remaining ingredients except the green onions.

Lower heat to simmer until fish is cooked. Turn off heat and stir in green onions. Serve over rice with French bread.

CHAPTER EIGHTEEN

Sunrise on Keith Lake

Sunrise on Keith Lake

The approximate hour of time that comprised what humans consider as sunrise was a magical time for a young lad on Keith Lake. All of the critters that operate only at night were retreating to their daytime hiding places, and the day creatures were beginning their activities for another day. By this time, all of the jobs surrounding my small bait enterprise were now completed, and it was time for thoughts of breakfast. Not just any breakfast, but my favorite thing to wake up to: Fried soft-shell blue crab. For the uninitiated, soft-shell crabs dipped in cornmeal and fried in hot oil are a welcome assault on the senses. A meal that is so rich and satisfying, that as a young lad I told my Mama that God must eat soft-shell crabs.

Blue crabs, like many crustaceans, have a soft tissue body surrounded by a calcium-based outer shell (exoskeleton). As the crab grows, the only way it can get bigger is to shed its outer shell, usually once or twice a year, and form a new one that is big enough for its enlarged body size. This activity takes about one day for the crab to accomplish. It is during the early part of the process, immediately after the outer shell splits and the crab exits, that the crab is most desirable for consumption. At this point, the body of the crab is extremely soft; so soft that locomotion is very slow, and its claws are so soft that it will not even attempt to bite you. The crab will usually hang on to a rock, piling or any submerged structure while the hardening process is occurring. The shoreline of my bait runs had plenty of underwater structures that were perfect for soft shelled crabs.

Every morning, as soon as there was enough light to see, I would begin my search around the rocks and other objects in the shallows of the shoreline with ever-heightening anticipation. It was rare to not find any soft-shell crabs. The norm was two or three, with the number increasing during the months of July thru September. I would immediately clean my catch and go back to the house, where I would find my Aunt Rita in the middle of preparing breakfast. Aunt Rita was a living contrast of the human experience. Her outward appearance was that of a simple person, usually dressed in an unassuming, home-made sift type dress, of which she possessed many in various colors of identical construction. I do not recall her ever wearing anything different, and under this she seldom wore anything else. She spoke in somewhat shortened sentences, and made facial gestures and off-looks to emphasize her message. Her opinions were many, and anything but simplistic. Often contradictory, she effortlessly moved from silence to social oratory at the drop of a hat, but she loved and liked me very much. Even though she appeared not to be close to anyone, I could tell by the look in her eyes and the way that she would take the time to do specific things for me that somehow, I had pierced the tough exterior that she worked so hard to fashion for herself and the world around her.

Aunt Rita was a marvel to behold. She would always take my soft-shell crabs and fry them just like I liked, without any positive or negative response, as if it were part of some organized routine. On the occasion that she felt that I had not cleaned them properly enough (for some arbitrary standard that she had developed), I would be forced to go back and re-clean them properly, and only when I had achieved this objective would she cook the crabs for me. This was so typically Aunt Rita. Even though her proclivities grated on the nerves of

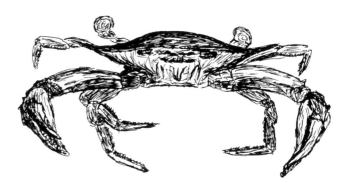

other people, her idiosyncrasies actually fascinated me, and endeared me in some strange celestial way. It was as if Aunt Rita's opinionated and abrupt statements were some sort of short-hand for a higher force or meaning which I would never be allowed to understand, but she always seemed to do some little thing that showed affection for me (like cooking my soft-shell crabs). As I think back about the time just before I actually ate the crabs, the sensation is so strong that it is as if I can actually "feel" the smell of my soft-shell crabs being cooked. With naïve exuberance, I would not hesitate to say that this was the best thing I ever ate, knowing full-well that any Cajun would readily say the same about many of the dishes they have eaten.

Like most of the really sensational food experiences I have had, the preparation was rather simple. The soft-shell crabs were lightly salted with a dash of cayenne pepper, rolled in coarse ground corn meal, fried in oil and turned only once. There was no profusion of ingredients and spices necessary (or even desirable) with soft-shell crabs. The crabs themselves provide the flavor, and the secret (if there is one) is in the execution. My dad used to say that when you fry seafood, you need enough oil to float the seafood, the oil needs to be hot, and you should only turn it once.

Fried Soft-shell Crabs

Having an abundance of soft-shell crabs to eat while I was growing up is truly a wondrous and delightful thing. To be able to virtually walk out of your door and find something so unexplainably delicious can only be described as magic. The joy of eating them is equally matched by the adventure of finding them amid the sights, sounds and aromas of nature in a place you call home. I also have had the privilege of indulging in fried soft-shell crabs cooked by two

different women in my life who were important to me: My Mama and
my Aunt Rita. It is so hard to decide which method of cooking soft-
shells was my favorite that I have decided to include both methods
of preparation; so that you, the reader, can try both and decide which
you prefer. At different points in my life, I have felt that I preferred
one over the other, but at this point in my life I remain immersed in a
rather pleasant quandary.

Aunt Rita's method of preparation was the simpler of the two, but
it was enhanced by the fact that she had access to very fresh, coarsely-
ground cornmeal which was secured by my Uncle George in a trade with
a person who owned a small mill. When I brought her my soft-shell
crabs after cleaning them to her satisfaction, Aunt Rita would simply
rinse them, sprinkle on some salt and a little dusting of cayenne pepper,
and completely coat them with corn meal. In a cast iron, dutch oven
bottom, she would pour in enough vegetable oil to deep-fry the soft-
shells until they were golden brown, and she would serve them to me.

Mama chose a slightly different track when she prepared soft-
shell crabs. Mama preferred to submerge the clean soft-shells in
a bowl of evaporated milk (which Mama called pet milk; probably
from a popular brand name), and then in the refrigerator for about
30 minutes to an hour. After that time, she would salt and pepper
the crabs, roll them in corn meal and deep fry in her deep cast
iron pot until golden brown. Mama would serve them to me with
Worcestershire sauce, and sometimes with a simple red sauce she made
with ketchup, Tabasco sauce and lemon juice.

When comparing the two methods employed by these two very
prominent women in my life, I have to say that both methods took
advantage of the inherent richness of soft-shell crabs to allow such
a basic preparation to evolve into such a magnificent assault on the
senses. In retrospect, I have to say that Aunt Rita's recipe was probably

enhanced by the ambiance of simply being on Keith Lake. Although I was probably oblivious to the fact at the time, I was somewhat hypnotized by all of the sensory elements that awaited me when I walked out of the door every morning on Keith Lake. As I searched for soft-shell crabs on the shore by Aunt Rita's house, I would be surrounded by the sound of the prevailing south-easterly wind off of the Gulf of Mexico that came with summer, as it whistled thru the salt grass and bull rushes. Even though it was omnipresent, the smell and taste of the salt air would still momentarily awaken you at irregular intervals to remind you of your surroundings and warm you with a somewhat odd form of security and well-being. I was joined in my search by all of my friends from the marsh. The *tchac* (pronounced *choc*, meaning blackbird) sings his song of the morning as he flits from the branches of the sea cane. A large blue *héron* (pronounced *a'rhon*, meaning heron), who ate breakfast with some degree of regularity with me along the shore, would occasionally raise his head with a small fish in his bill that he had just caught still protruding, as if to say "good morning, Jim – good luck with your catch." I often felt that we were friends since he would occasionally let me approach him, but he never let me get too close. While constantly staring at me with his very large eye, the blue heron would seem to trust me to a point – some interval that only he knew the distance. The small fiddler

Héron

237

crabs would scurry ahead of
me along the shore, and duck
into their holes in the bank
as if they believed me to be a
threat. I sometimes mused to
myself that you would think by
now that they would know that

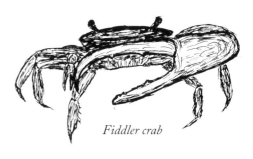

Fiddler crab

I was not there to harm them. Such was the wonderland of my youth,
the remembrance of which comforts me as the light at the end my
tunnel burns brighter. It was a gift of life that I thought everyone had
at the time, but I now know was specially crafted only for me.

Today, I get soft-shell crabs like you will have to – by buying
them from a seafood vendor (when you can find them). They also do
not keep well, even when frozen, unless they have been frozen totally
immersed in water when they were very freshly caught. I have a recipe
that was based upon both Mama's and Aunt Rita's that I now use, and
with which I am very satisfied. I hope that you will try this one, and I
sincerely hope that you enjoy it as much as I have throughout my life.

INGREDIENTS:

4	Soft-shell crabs, cleaned
1 can	Evaporated milk
4 cups	Coarse ground corn meal *(stone ground is si bon)*
	Salt to taste
	Cayenne pepper to taste

About one hour before you plan to begin cooking, place the
cleaned soft-shell crabs in a bowl with the evaporated milk. I like to
add the cayenne pepper to the evaporated milk and stir it well before I
add in the soft-shell crabs. I then place the bowl in the refrigerator for
a least ½ hour prior to cooking.

Select a cooking vessel that is deep (like a cast iron, dutch oven bottom), so that you can pour in about two or three inches of oil and still have sufficient height left to contain the bubbling oil during frying.

Begin heating the oil over high heat until a temperature of about 360 deg. F is attained (a frying thermometer is recommended). While the oil is heating, pour the cornmeal into a large baking pan (I use a 9" X 13"). Remove the crabs from the refrigerator and begin battering them in preparation for frying using the "wet hand/dry hand" method. I would recommend only frying two crabs at one time, since they cook rather quickly and it is best to not overload the cooking vessel. As we have discussed in the past, it is important to remember that in order to maintain the proper cooking temperature, you have to have some battered crabs ready to immediately put in when you take the cooked crabs out. As you take the soft-shell crabs out of the oil, place them on paper towels to absorb the excess oil and salt to taste while they are still very hot.

CHAPTER NINETEEN

My Blue (Crab) Heaven

My Blue (Crab) Heaven

The Atlantic blue crab, *Callinectes sapidus* (from the Greek *calli* meaning beautiful and *nectes* meaning swimmer), is the proper name for the blue crab species that every Cajun spends a great portion of his life pursuing and eating. The Atlantic blue crab, or common blue crab, is a decapod crab of the swimming crab family *Portunidae* that ranges along the western edge of the Atlantic Ocean from Cape Cod in the northern hemisphere, to as far south as Argentina in the southern hemisphere. This, of course, includes the entire coast of the Gulf of Mexico, which is where Cajuns got so intimately involved with blue crabs. Blue crabs have been known to grow to a carapace width of 9 inches, which requires multiple molting stages to accomplish, since the exoskeleton is rigid and must be "shed" to allow a new and larger exoskeleton to form. Growth and molting are profoundly influenced by food availability, temperature, salinity and other factors in the blue crab's environment. These same factors also influence the complex reproduction cycles of the blue crab, which occur in varying stages of water salinity. A female blue crab will mate once in her lifetime in the fresh, brackish waters of inland estuaries, but she must travel to higher salinity levels in offshore waters to hatch her offspring which can number up to 2 million per brood. With such a large number of blue crabs being born so often throughout the bayous of Louisiana and Texas and the rest of the Gulf of Mexico, it causes one to wonder why we are not completely overrun with blue crabs. Then, wrapped in the warm glow of enlightenment, you finally understand that the good Lord created the Cajun people to keep the population of blue crabs in check.

Having grown up a bayou Cajun and on Keith Lake, I inherited a working knowledge of blue *costeau* (pronounced *coo sto'*, meaning male crab). The name "blue crab" comes from the distinct blue color on the lower edge of the male crabs' claws. The female blue crab has a red-orange coloring along the lower edge of her claws. As male blue crabs age, the points of their claws and the teeth on them get progressively rounded, making the bite more painful, bruising (but usually not breaking) the skin. Female blue crabs have smaller claws with sharper teeth, especially when they are younger, that are more likely to break the skin and cause bleeding. This of course is exacerbated by the reflex to sling the crab off of you when you are bitten, thereby enlarging the gash and making a bad situation worse. To the uninitiated, crabs seem impossible to deal with on any practical basis, but after working with them for a while and learning their physical limitations, you learn how to handle them and how to avoid getting bitten. Blue crabs are very quick and strong creatures, and have the ability to inflict very painful bites. They should only be handled by people skilled in their handling, or with the proper equipment (crab tongs) and much care.

As a child, I worked predominately in the crab part of the seafood business of my aunt and uncle's on Keith Lake. They sold crabs by the dozen, and my job was to catch them, which I did in abundance. When I was growing up in the 50's, commercial crabbing was usually done by people who had grown up in a family of people engaged in commercial crabbing. Commercial crabbing was nowhere near as widespread (and over-fished) as it is today. Back then, crabs were abundant everywhere, but especially in Keith Lake, since only my family was allowed to crab and shrimp there. Crabs were so prevalent that my aunt would have to order a halt to my catching activities when I had filled up our holding boxes, which I could easily do. We had

Aunt Rita and Uncle George LaBove, circa 1952

four holding boxes that were each about eight feet long by about 4 feet wide, and about 5 feet deep. They were constructed of a wooden frame, onto which many small "slats" (thin boards about 2 inches wide) were nailed, leaving about a ¼ inch crack between them to allow water to flow in and out but not let the crabs escape. These holding boxes were suspended into about four feet of water from the edge of the wharf, on cables that were wrapped around a piece of pipe with crossed bars affixed to the ends, so that the boxes could be raised and lowered into the water. When fully lowered into the water, each box was designed to hold about fifty to sixty dozen crabs, depending upon the size (medium to large crabs). One of the boxes was reserved strictly for large male crabs which brought the best price: Fifty cents per dozen.

One box was reserved for large female crabs, which some people (especially Cajuns) preferred, and they were thirty-five cents per dozen. Then, the remaining two boxes were for medium and up, male/female mixed, and they brought twenty-five cents per dozen. Aunt Rita paid me *cinq sous* (pronounced *sayn soo*, meaning five cents) per dozen. On any given weekend, we would sell completely out, but I would have the boxes filled up again within a day or two. My aunt was constantly on me for not keeping count of the crabs I put into the holding boxes, and for putting in too many.

There were so many crabs in Keith Lake back then that within a minute of returning the drop nets into the water, there would be more crabs in them. I had out about 15 to 20 drop nets along the wharf that I ran constantly all day long. In addition, I had a line attached from the end of the wharf to a telephone pole that was about 250 to 300 feet away in the water that had crab bait suspended about every eight feet or so. I would kneel in the front of my *pirogue* (pronounced *pee' row*, meaning a small home-made boat) and pull myself along the line with a hand net; I would catch the crabs and simply drop them into the floor of the pirogue. By the time I got to the pole and turned my pirogue around to come back, there would already be crabs on the baits again. When I got back to the wharf, I could pole my pirogue over to the holding tanks, sort the sizes into the proper tank and then go out again. I had to maintain a constant vigilance working around the wharf in my pirogue, because the *serpent congo* (pronounced *serra phah kan go*,

Serpent congo

meaning water moccasin) would sometimes coil up on the cross-arms between the posts to sun themselves, and occasionally an alligator would be lurking under the wharf. To an alligator, a serpent congo sunning himself on the cross-arms was like a "link on a stick" at the fair.

To the average couch potato, this all seems like a lot of work coupled with "more than I bargained for" danger attached, and I have to admit that as I write about those times, they do sound inordinately troublesome. In reality, none of

Canard

this was the case. At the time, I remember those as being fun times of discovery and adventure. The bulk of my Keith Lake experiences occurred during the ages of roughly 4 to about 17 years of age. In addition to the fact that bayou Cajuns are raised to work in the family business as a part of life, the house on Keith Lake was miles from any other people, and there were no other people my age. I grew up watching the *rat musqué* (pronounced *ra' miskay* – muskrat) and *fouine* (pronounced *foo'ein* – mink) in the marshes. I swam in the water watching *canard* (pronounced *kan' nar* – duck) and *aigrette* (pronounced *aah grett'* – egret) do their daily jobs along the shoreline at the edge of the marsh. I learned that the alligator and the water moccasin, for the most part, were not there to do harm to me, as long as I did not interrupt the natural order of things. For instance, bayou Cajuns did not have to be told not to feed the alligators, because they knew that there is no such thing as a friendly alligator. Bayou Cajuns also knew to avoid the part of the marsh where alligators were nesting during mating season, since alligators were particularly testy when they were in love. As far as the *serpent congo* was concerned, you just knew to give them their space. There was a certain part of your brain that was always on duty and that subconsciously watched for water moccasins, seeming to know where they liked to lurk. With some observation, you grew to know that a water moccasin did not awaken with the intent to bite the first person he encountered on that day. The observations I made growing up in the marshes gave me a sense that all things in nature had a way that they performed their daily tasks just to get by in life. Nature, with her sometimes cruel efficiency, kept everybody's population in check, and things actually worked very well as long as you didn't interfere.

Cora's Stuffed Crab and Crab Patties

Cora always made the absolute best Cajun-style crab patties and stuffed crabs. The stuffing recipe is the same for both dishes – only the presentation is different. When you want a dish that looks authentically Cajun, then stuffed crabs using the crab back to stuff is the way to go. If you just want to eat something simply wonderful, then you will surely appreciate the crab patties. Mama was always adamant about the amount of bread crumbs that were used in this dish. She said that you should <u>never</u> exceed more than one part bread crumbs to four parts crab meat. She usually did not even use nearly that much bread crumbs, since crab meat was something that we always had in abundance. I have found Cora's bread crumb limit to be a red line, and I consider it an axiom in my dishes that use crab meat stuffing. This recipe has become one of my family favorites. As Cotton would exclaim, "you talk about good." Like almost all of Cora's dishes, the simplicity is the most striking feature.

Cora's Stuffed Crabs

INGREDIENTS

For stuffing:

4 cups	Lump blue crab meat (other species of crab meat will work)
1/2 cup	Bread crumbs* (<u>at most</u> - less is better)
2	Eggs (beaten)
1-1½ cup	Chopped green onion tops
1 stick	Melted butter (salted)
1 tbsp.	Lemon juice
2 cups	Corn meal

If serving stuffed crabs:

6-10	Crab backs (depending upon size) that have been retained from boiled crabs, cleaned and brushed or any small ramekin type of dishes will suffice.

In a bowl, gently combine crab meat, bread crumbs, lemon juice and green onions, trying not to break up crab meat too much. Beat eggs and gently combine into mixture. Drizzle melted butter while folding into mixture. Refrigerate mixture for at least 30 minutes, or until very cold. Keeping the mixture cold until cooking helps it hold together during the frying process.

For Stuffed Crabs: Pack stuffing mixture into crab backs (or ramekins) and coat with corn meal. Fry stuffed crab backs in 375 deg. F canola oil until golden brown. Salt while hot (if desired) to desired salinity. Stuffed ramekins can be baked in a 375 deg. F oven until golden brown – usually about 30 to 40 minutes, depending on the size ramekin used. I once used large, crab meat-stuffed oyster shells leveled up in a bed of rock salt for a stunning presentation. Stuffed crab backs can also be baked if desired, although frying is the most Cajun presentation.

For Crab Patties: Remove stuffing mixture from refrigerator and form into patties, about 1" thick and as big in diameter as desired. Press into corn meal and fully coat (including edges), placing on a waxed paper covered cooking sheet. Refrigerate until time to cook (or until grease gets hot). Fry in 375 deg. F canola oil until golden brown. Salt while hot (if needed) to desired salinity.

Bread Crumbs: In a 250 deg. F oven, toast 8-10 slices of bread (whole wheat) until very hard. Crumble until a fine consistency and it should yield more than enough.

Cotton's Smoked Blue Crabs

Cotton's old oil drum outdoor cooker was often pressed into service for other cooking ventures. Occasionally, when the shrimp were not running very well and we had the occasion to be back at the house earlier than usual, my sisters and I would push on Cotton to smoke us some crabs. I guess that by now you have probably decided that I have quite a few "favorite" dishes, since I seem to tell you that everything is my favorite. Probably, I just miss my Mama and Daddy quite a bit, and as I grow older, I remember these dishes for the warmth that they projected to me from them. I have cooked smoked crabs the way that my Daddy cooked them for my children, and they are very fond of them as well. If you like crabs as much as I do, then this dish will probably become one of your favorites as well.

The thing that makes this dish so superb is the smoke from sassafras heartwood, but I have used other woods, and they have been good. Sassafras wood for smoking was my Daddy's favorite, especially for seafood, but it is admittedly difficult to locate in today's market place.

Cotton's Smoked Blue Crabs

INGREDIENTS:

24   Large blue crabs (cleaned and brushed with legs and claws attached)
1   Stick of butter
    Cayenne pepper (to taste)
    Salt (to taste)
2 – 3   Chunks of hardwood (for smoke)
1 bag   Lump charcoal

At least one hour prior to cooking, you should begin soaking your hardwood chunks with water to retard them from flaming during cooking. You simply want them to emit smoke continuously.

To cook this dish properly, you will need an outdoor cooker with a lid (and bottom and top smoke control valves - gates) to hold in the smoke. Light the lump charcoal (preferably with an electric lighter and without the use of charcoal lighter) sufficient to build up a bed of hot coals. When the coals are hot and ready, place the water-soaked hardwood chunks 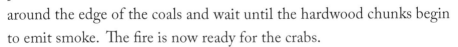 around the edge of the coals and wait until the hardwood chunks begin to emit smoke. The fire is now ready for the crabs.

Salt and pepper (cayenne) the tops of the crabs to taste and add a small dab of butter to the cavity of each crab. Place them right-side-up on the grill about 6 to 8 inches from the hot coals. Replace the lid to begin cooking and smoking. Cook about 4 to 5 minutes per side, depending upon how hot the fire is and remove from grill. Remember that crabs cook rather quickly. Serve hot.

A word of caution: After you try this dish once, on the next try, you will be tempted to increase the amount of butter that you put into the cavity prior to placing the crabs on the grill. You only want enough butter to permeate the crab body and flavor it. If you add too much butter, you will increase the risk of the coals flaming up when you turn the crabs over to cook on the other side. At this point, I feel quite sure that you do not see the need to ask me how I know this.

CHAPTER TWENTY

"And One Day, I Left the Salt Marshes..."

"And One Day, I Left the Salt Marshes…"

The salt marshes whisper to you in many ways. Red-winged *tchac* flit about with their soft chirps, announcing to their friends and lovers their location. The dry sea cane leaves rub against each other in the gentle salt air breeze, occasionally interrupted by the patter of the quick, splashing feet of the *poul deau* (pronounced *poole' do* and is the Cajun name for a "coot") as it scrambles to flight from the water of a marsh pot hole. Frogs seem to be constantly singing their love songs, from the cricket-like click of the smallest green frog to the fog horn bellow of the bull frog. These and other familiar sounds of the bayous and salt marshes were about to fade as I reached the age where a person begins to wonder what life might hold for them. What is it like out there? Surely I am bound for greatness, fame, fortune…

At the age of seventeen, having just completed high school, I decided that it was time for me to go and seek out whatever was in store for me. About two months into my first year at a local junior college, I abruptly quit and signed up to "ship out" with a labor

Poul deau

union, with which a friend of mine had connections. My first (and what was to be my only) job was to be assigned to the deck department on a ship called the Steel Designer, a C-3 cargo ship bound for the Persian Gulf. I remained on the ship for seven months, traveling to stops including: Beirut, Lebanon; Alexandria, Egypt; Saudi Arabia; Jordan and the Gulf of Aqaba; Iran and Iraq (Basra); Bombay (now Mumbai), India; and finally Cádiz and Alicante, Spain. Apparently, all of this was sufficient for me to realize that I was on the wrong path, so I re-entered college life upon my return to the United States.

Dodie as a New Orleans Saints Cheerleader, circa 1978

In 1967, while I was in my junior year at Lamar State College of Technology (currently Lamar University), I started a music store called The Guitar & Banjo Studio, which I owned and operated for about 20 years or so before moving on to other pursuits. During that time, I also graduated from Lamar with a double major in History and English. It was only after years of other ventures that I finally came to know that I was not destined for greatness, fame or fortune; at least, not the Kardashian type. I did, however, achieve all such things through the people I grew to love and with whom I associated. With maturity, a person discovers that only through family, confidants and friends can a person ever really achieve greatness. For ordinary folks, fame and fortune only results from raising good children that go on to be happy in their pursuits and comfortable with themselves.

In the spring of 1980, I met and subsequently married Dorothy ("Dodie") Lynn Lambert from New Orleans, Louisiana. Dodie's fifteen minutes of fame came from the fact that she was cheerleader for the New Orleans Saints football team during the 1978-79 seasons. By all outward appearances, I had "married above myself" as a friend of mine had remarked, but I just looked at it as if I was simply a good salesman. Dodie and I had two sons, James LaBove and Garret LaBove. James owns and operates his own graphic design/advertising business, Inks, Inc. d/b/a Spindletop.net, and Garret is currently in the very final stages of attaining his Ph.D. in Power Engineering, a field of electrical engineering.

Dodie and I raised our children to enjoy and appreciate their Cajun heritage and its foods and activities. Even though both of the boys are grown and in pursuit of their own endeavors, we still find time to go crabbing and fishing, and take vacations that include crabbing and fishing when we can all find the time to do so. We have done our best to expose our children to many Cajun ideas and practices so that they will not disappear, because we both believe that the Cajun life

James and Garret in Grand Isle, Louisiana, circa 2000

James and Garret with a haul of red fish, 2015

has worth and needs to be preserved, while allowing life in general to continue and evolve. I can't speak for the entire Cajun people, but for me, being a Cajun made me what I am today, and for that I am eternally grateful.

I am finally at a stage in life of insightfulness and reflection. In looking back, I can re-live (and re-invent) my successes, and insert Clint Eastwood quotations into those embarrassing moments when such words somehow eluded me as I tried to squirm my way out of them. As men age, they begin to talk about the magnitude of their early abilities and accomplishments, as well as "when I was younger, I could (lift, carry, climb, hold, eat or whatever boastful accomplishment – real or otherwise) you could imagine." This brings to mind an appropriate quote made during one such conversation with a good friend, Ed Batton. In response to one of my usual stretched recollections, he gazed out as if in deep thought, dramatically sighed at the weight of it all, and finally said in a mock stoic tone, "I never was the man I once was."

Dodie doing what she loves the most, circa 2010

James with the catch of the day

Garret reeling in a big one

Garret, Dodie and James at the "Blessing of the Fleet"

Dodie as a cheerleader, circa 1978

Dis is a real coonass, Sha'

la fin

Index of Recipes
Listed alphabetically

References

The following references are acknowledged regarding the production of this book:

Brasseaux, Carl A., "The Founding of New Arcadia: The Beginnings of Acadian Life in Louisiana, 1765 – 1803." Baton Rouge: Louisiana State University Press.

Brasseaux, Carl A., "Acadian to Cajun: Transformation of a People." Jackson Mississippi: University Press of House.

John Mack Faragher (2005). "A Great and Noble Scheme: The Tragic Story of the Expulsion of the French Acadians from their American Homeland." New York: W.W. Norton.

"A Letter by Jean-Baptiste Semer, an Acadian in New Orleans, to His Father in Le Havre, April 20, 1766." Translated by Bey Grieve. Louisiana History (Spring 2007).

Varela, Beatiz, "The Lexicon of Marie Laveau's Voodoo," The University of New Orleans, page 4.

Muncy, Robert J., 1954. "White Shrimp." Species profiles: Life histories and environmental requirements of coastal fishes and invertebrates (South Atlantic). United States Fish and wildlife Service. FW/WS/OBS-82/11.27., pp. 1 thru 19.

Riekerk, G. "Commercial Fisheries: Shrimp." "Characterization of the Ashepoo-Combahee-Edisto (ACE) Basin, South Carolina." National Oceanic and Atmospheric Administration.

Burukovsky (1997), "Selection of a type species for *Farfantepenaeus* Burukovsky (Ctustacca: Decapoda: *Penaeidae*)." Proceedings of the Biological Society of Washington 110(1): 154.

Ives, J. E. (1891. "Crustacea from the northern coast of Yucatan, the harbor of Vera Cruz, the west coast of Florida and the Bermuda Islands." Proceedings of the Academy of Natural Sciences of Philadelphia 43:176-207. JSTOR 4061707.

"Oyster Reefs: Ecological Importance." US National Oceanic and Atmospheric Administration.

Newell R. (2004). "Ecosystem Influences of Natural and Cultivated Populations of Suspensions-Feeding Bivalve Molluses: A Review." J. Shellfish Research 23(1):51-61.

"Oyster Farming in Louisiana." Louisiana State University.

"Oyster Restoration Projected to Provide Significant Boost to Bay Grasses While Removing Nitrogen Pollution from the Bay." Maryland Department of Natural Resources.

"1978-2007: Louisiana Summary of Agriculture and Natural Resources." Louisiana State University Agricultural Center, Baton Rouge, Louisiana (2009).

Walls, Jerry g. (2009). "Crawfishes of Louisiana." Baton Rouge, Louisiana: Florida State University Press. ISBN 978-0-8071-3409-2.

Huxley, Thomas Henry (1880). "The Crayfish: an Introduction to the Study of Zoology." New York: D. Appleton & Co.

"Maryland State Crustacean." Maryland State Archives.

Williams, A. B.(1974). "The Swimming Crabs of the Genus *Callinectes* (Decapoda: *Portunidae*)." Fishery Bulletin. 72(3): 685-692.

"*Callinectes similis* Lesser Blue Crab." Smithsonian Marine Station at Fort Pierce.

"Blue Crab. *Callinectes Sapidus*." Maryland Fish Facts: Maryland Department of Natural Resources. April 4, 2007.

"*Callinectes Sapidus.*" Smithsonian Marine Station at Fort Pierce. October 11, 2004.

Millikin, Mark. R.; Williams, Austin B. (March 1984). "Synopsis of Biological Data on the Blue Crab *Callinectes Sapidus* Rathburn." National Oceanic and Atmospheric Administration Technical Report NMRS 1: 1-32

LaFleur, Amanda, "A Cajun French-English Glossary." Louisiana State University. www.lsu.edu/hss/french/undergraduate_program/cajun_french_english_glossary.php

Select drawings from this book now available for purchase as signed art prints!

AN ILLUSTRATED LOOK INTO CAJUN LIFE

Need the perfect piece of wall art for your Cajun home or beach cabin? We're pleased to offer a selection of Jim's signed illustrations as gorgeous matted prints, ready for framing.

Jim's illustrations are imprinted on archival-quality 140-pound watercolor paper through a giclée ink transfer, all done in-house by the Cotton's Seafood team. We package the prints with a sturdy backer board and your choice of mat color.

Visit our online store today to learn more and pick up a unique glimpse into mid-century bayou Cajun life!

VISIT OUR SHOP AT WWW.COTTONS-SEAFOOD.COM

Offering a wide variety of unique Cajun gifts:

BOOKS • ART PRINTS • MUGS • POSTCARDS • APPAREL • AND MORE!

Join our mailing list for the latest updates and specials!

Blue Pelican

PUBLICATIONS

We specialize in books celebrating untold stories in
Cajun history. Some of our other titles include:

COTTON'S SEAFOOD

A CAJUN AUTOBIOGRAPHICAL COOKBOOK

SKETCHES OF MY
Cajun Life
VOLUME 1

Sunrise over Keith Lake

A Cajun Autobiographical Cookbook

Learn more, preview, and purchase our titles here:

OUR ONLINE SHOP	OUR PUBLISHER'S SITE	ALSO AVAILABLE ON
COTTONS-SEAFOOD.COM	BLUEPELICANPUBLICATIONS.COM	AMAZON.COM

For the latest news on *Cotton's Seafood* and related projects, visit our website:

www.cottons-seafood.com

Or find us on Facebook: **f** /CottonsSeafoodBook

55400897R00171

Made in the USA
Columbia, SC
13 April 2019